China, Taiwan, Japan, the United States, and the World

Edited by
Kenneth W. Thompson

Series Editor
Shao-chuan Leng

Volume V
The Miller Center Series
on Asian Political Leadership

UNIVERSITY
PRESS OF
AMERICA

Lanham • New York • Oxford

The Miller Center

University of Virginia

Copyright © 1998 by
University Press of America,® Inc.
4720 Boston Way
Lanham, Maryland 20706

12 Hid's Copse Rd.
Cummor Hill, Oxford OX2 9JJ

Copublished by arrangement with
The Miller Center of Public Affairs,
University of Virginia

The views expressed by the author(s) of this publication do not necessarily represent the opinions of the Miller Center. We hold to Jefferson's dictum that: "Truth is the proper and sufficient antagonist to error, and has nothing to fear from the conflict, unless by human interposition, disarmed of her natural weapons, free argument and debate."

Library of Congress Cataloging-in-Publication Data

China, Taiwan, Japan, the United States, and the world / Edited by Kenneth
W. Thompson.
p. cm.—(Miller Center series on Asian Political leadership ; v. 5)
1. East Asia—Relations—Foreign countries. 2. China. I. Thompson,
Kenneth W. II. Series.
DS518.1.C4926   1997   303.48'25—DC21   971-42721 CIP

ISBN: 0-7618-0989-9 (cloth: alk. ppr.)
ISBN: 0-7618-0990-2 (pbk: alk. ppr.)

TO

TONY AND NORA LENG

Table of Contents

III. PATTERNS, PERSPECTIVES, AND PRINCIPLES

IV. CHINA AND BEYOND

Preface

Thanks to Professor Shao-chuan Leng, Asia has emerged as a field of study for the Miller Center. His influence on the field is reflected in numerous graduate students who come to the University of Virginia for Asian studies. Most come because they know of Professor Leng's reputation or have heard of the role he has played in the study of China and Taiwan.

Under the heading of a major topic for forums and studies, we have included Asian countries and governance. Our primary interest has been China and Taiwan, Japan, Southeast Asia, and a few smaller countries. Recognized authorities have visited the Miller Center, conducted forums, or taken part in colloquia or conferences.

Miller Center conferences on Asia has resulted in the following publications: *Changes in China: Party, State, and Society* (1989); *Coping with Crises: How Governments Deal with Emergencies* (1990); *Chiang Ching-Kuo's Leadership in the Development of the Republic of China on Taiwan* (1993); and *Reform and Development in Deng's China* (1994). Presentations and papers by individual scholars and policymakers appear in the Miller Center series on constitutionalism in *The U.S. Constitution and the Constitutions of Asia* (1988). Distinguished Asian guests have discussed arms control and governance. Their chapters appear in books with that title. Asia is part of our program.

Finally, we are engaged in completing arrangements for the creation of the C. K. Yen Chair, dealing with political leadership in Taiwan, China, and Asia. President Yen was the father of Nora Leng, Professor Leng's able and charming wife. The creation of the chair assures the continuation of the study of leadership in China and Taiwan for years to come. It makes possible a comparative dimension that would otherwise not exist in Miller Center programs.

Introduction

The first essay in Part I is by Robert J. Myers, former publisher of *The New Republic*. Dr. Myers was in residence at the Miller Center and the University of Virginia, where he taught in the Government and Foreign Affairs Department. For over a decade he was president of the Carnegie Council on Ethics and International Affairs, where he created a scholarly journal on ethics and international affairs. His background on Asia includes long familiarity with China and Korea. In his presentation, he analyzes Chinese politics, the military and the Chinese economy. He enters into the debate over economic reform without political liberalization. He discusses the significance of the recognition of South Korea by China. As is often the case in discussions of China, he turns early to the relationship of China and Japan. Inevitably, the relation of China to the Association of Southeast Asian Nations (ASEAN) countries comes to the fore as well as the United States' relation with them. He concludes that China is likely to be dominant in that region for the next couple of decades. As for its economy, China surpasses the other countries of Asia in its growth, and Myers looks at specific regions and cities. He reviews Taiwan's position in the region and its relationship with the United States. On the question of U.S. sales of advanced military fighters to Taiwan, he rejects the idea that it could lead to war with China.

The second chapter is by Professor Leng, who appears to be in agreement with Myers on a number of issues. In the beginning of his chapter, he reviews the history of Taiwan's relation with China. In particular he traces the democratization of Taiwan, which obviously sets it apart from China. Leng asks and responds to the questions: What are Taiwan's main problems? What are its ethnic divisions and how has it sought to manage these differences in the governance of the country? He traces the various stages in China's relations with Taiwan and lists its most recent manifestations. Leng discusses the enormous expansion of economic relations between

Taiwan and China. Taiwan at the time he wrote had a $14 billion trade surplus with China and had trade via Hong Kong of $17 billion. Despite these remarkable economic statistics they have not achieved a political breakthrough. Taiwan has international relations with some 30 countries, most of them smaller states. Its cultural relations are more extensive. The country's greatest achievement is its economic growth. Its per capita GNP is $12,000 with a foreign reserve exchange of $100 million. These and other key issues form the substance of Leng's chapter.

Professor Brantly Womack of the University of Virginia's Department of Government and Foreign Affairs examines China and Southeast Asia after the Cold War. He takes a broad view of the problem, excluding some of the details that can only be considered in a whole series of essays. He reviews the patterns of relations between countries in the region in the 1950s compared with the 1990s. Hostility between present-day China and Vietnam began to develop in the 1970s. Womack discovers the cause for this development in three factors: unrealistic expectations of what victory in the Vietnam War would bring; the possibility of Vietnam's alliance with the Soviet Union, which appears to be a more attractive choice than China; and China's support of the Khmer Rouge in Cambodia and the resulting Vietnamese invasion of Cambodia. With the end of the Vietnam War, any Soviet threat disappeared. The region took on a new pattern of Asia for Asians. The region's main characteristic was not military crises but economic progress. The region has taken on increasing importance for China as its exports within the region increased to a point where they equaled its exports to the United States. China's importance for the region has grown dramatically. Womack concludes with a review of possible problems in the region, among them Chinese nationalism, control over the Spratly Islands and therefore 80 percent of the South China Sea, and competition between China and Japan. He sees danger for countries like Vietnam if the United States were to withdraw from the region and eliminate its balancing role vis-à-vis China.

The next chapter in Part I is a colorful account of the advance preparations and implementation of Nixon's historic journey to China by two engaging personalities. It is the story of the technological and human problems that arose in facilitating the visit. It required travel, logistics, and coordinating a team of 100 Americans—television crews, technicians, aircraft crews, secret service—in three separate trips to the region. It entailed decisions on how to configure and manage the historic mission of forging an opening China's relations with the United States. It introduces famous Chinese counterparts in the enterprise, including Ambassador Han Hsu and Zhou Enlai. The Walkers report on the attitudes of the Chinese and their request for information for their manuals on every piece of equipment brought into China. For the participants, the mission was conducted in freezing February Peking weather without movies or television or even enjoying a walk without Chinese surveillance. This essay provides a delightful interlude in writings that otherwise concentrate on hard political and economic questions.

Following the Walkers, three distinguished scholars and diplomats offer their impressions on China in the 1990s. Professors John Armitage, Inis Claude, and Shao-chuan Leng provide firsthand perspectives on China viewed from differing backgrounds and experiences. They were impressed by China's quest for prestige and recognition as the site of the Olympics in 2000. All were impressed by the vitality of Shanghai. They find that CNN and China's communication with the world has made the totalitarianism of the 1940s unlikely to repeat itself. China is proud of 3,000 years of history and culture. Its values and beliefs are more complex than most Americans understand. One observer pictures the incredible bicycle traffic. He notes the co-existence of Confucianism, Buddhism, and Taoism and the relative absence of religious wars. He compares China's and Russia's confidence in their own beliefs but also notes possible sources of internal tension that could lead to aggressive nationalism. A third observer calls attention to the substitution of China's version of "socialist-market economy" for a "planned economy as the basis of their economics." After enumerating many of China's problems, he indicates why the Chinese nonetheless have the ability to cope.

Part II introduces another major player in the future of international politics in Asia, namely, Japan. Chalmers Johnson, who had a significant role in the University of California during

Berkeley's rise to preeminence in Asian studies, lays bare some of the contradictions in Japanese-American relations. His primary thesis is that the Asian scene is changing, but no one is facing up to these changes. Although Asians talk of Asia for the Asians, they simultaneously implore the United States to remain involved in the region. At international conferences such as those held at Shimoda, they talk of "Asia for the Asians" and the "restoration of Asia," yet they urge a continued American military presence without offering any reason why the United States has this responsibility. Yet Japan is disengaging from the United States. Johnson sets forth the evidence. Today, Japan's trade surplus with other East Asian countries exceeds that with the United States. Johnson points to three developing trends in U.S.-Japan relations. First, Japan's opinion makers are preparing the country for a change in their international relationships, whether they wish it or not. Second, China has begun to assert itself through its economic power over overseas Chinese and non-Asian investors intended to balance Japan's actual and potential power. Third, evidence of a drift in U.S. foreign policy is growing. It reflects inertia in military deployments and political expediency in responding to domestic politics.

Asian observers are waiting for an incident that will reveal how much the world balance of power has shifted to Asia and how little prepared Americans are for meeting this change. Neither the Americans nor the East Asians understand why the Americans are still in Okinawa and why 37,000 frontline troops remain in Korea. Americans fail to recognize that nearly all conflicts are regional and by assuming a Sparta-like role as a global policeman, the United States risks geostrategic irrelevance. Japan for its part continues to behave like an export-oriented developing country tied by a 1951 treaty to the United States. Yet it has for the first time in history a $100 billion account surplus. Johnson goes on to analyze China's and Japan's rise to dominance in the region and beyond. Johnson explores the implications of these factors for the future of world politics.

The final essay in Part II discusses the relations of Japan and the United States in light of Japan's economic reforms. In brief, those reforms include deregulation, changes in their electoral systems and a tax-cut stimulus package. The three issues that Anderson discusses in U.S.-Japan relations are the personal relations between the Japanese prime minister and President Clinton and U.S. diplomats, U.S.-Japanese security relations, and economic trade relations between the two countries. Both countries must eventually determine the extent to which changing circumstances require fundamental changes in their perspectives and policies.

Part III directs attention to the patterns of life in Asian countries, the perspectives of the people, and the principles by which they govern their lives. Professor Shaozhong Pan is the former dean of the Foreign Affairs College in Beijing. Instead of approaching human rights in a polemical and contentious mode, he examines them from a historical cross-cultural perspective. He points out the different views of human rights, emphasizing either their individualistic or collective character. He traces their rooting in political or economic factors. He quotes John Dewey on the function and reality of culture: "The idea that human nature is inherently and exclusively individual is itself a product of a cultural, individualistic movement." Moreover, individual rights may be either economic, social, or political. Islam, Hinduism, and Buddhism have not had a tradition of individuality. Pan traces the idea of human rights in other religions, including the Judeo-Christian religion, and compares human rights in China with the American or West European idea. In China, rights find a basis in secularism. In Confucian teaching, the people as a whole are the foundation of the country, but this idea is different from the Western concept of democracy. The Buddhist concept of mercy is fundamental. Dr. Pan analyzes the Communist period, especially after 1949, with regard to human rights. As few if any Chinese observers have done, Dr. Pan helps us understand the differences between the fundamental basis of human rights in China and the West, linking it with culture and economics.

Caibo Wang is one of the founders of political science at Jilin University in China. My colleague, James Sterling Young, met her on a United States Information Agency trip to China. She first came to the United States as a visiting scholar at Rutgers University. In an exceedingly well-written paper entitled "China's

Model of Development," she sets out to explain the vast changes in China's economy and looks ahead to the future. First, she relates the facts regarding its dramatic changes. Second, she explains the reasons for the Chinese government's adopting the model. She examines China's historic policies and current status. Next she explores lessons that can be drawn from the U.S.S.R.'s experiments. Finally, she considers development in the Eastern European countries. Her review is a masterpiece of clear and lucid analysis dealing first with agricultural decentralization, then the rise of small entrepreneurs, next fiscal decentralization, the creation of special economic zones, and finally, the introduction of a dual price system and a dual foreign currency exchange system. She goes on to examine the impact of reform and development on Chinese society, emphasizing the opening up of the Chinese people's view of the world. She explodes the myth that the predevelopment Chinese people were the happiest people in the world. She demonstrates how much better conditions have become. Not everyone has benefited as yet, however, and she discusses the unfinished business of economic reform. She traces the impact of economic change, especially on certain aspects of the political system. Finally, she delves into the details of China's model for economic development and in particular the differences with countries such as the Soviet Union. She concludes with a discussion of possible problems and solutions.

Dr. Cheng-yi Lin is one of the University of Virginia's most successful graduate students in government and foreign affairs. He is a research fellow at one of the world's most famous institutes, the Academia Sinica. In Chapter 10 he analyzes the New World Order and Taiwan's changing international role. He offers an approach to foreign policy that emphasizes decisionmakers, the domestic structure of a country, and the international system. Within this framework, he explains the evolution of Taiwan's policies. He goes on to assess more broadly Taiwan's abnormal international status and its methods of foreign policy. Lastly, he analyzes Taiwan's approach to the world in terms of functionalism in international relations and the informal relations that have gone on between Taiwan and China. Development and trade have been a strong point in Taiwan's approach to the world. Dr. Lin concludes with a discussion of Taiwan's nonmembership association with the United Nations. His perspective is sound both from a theoretical and structural standpoint. In the discussion period, Lin answers a wide range of questions, all bearing on Taiwan's relations with the world.

Chalmers Johnson contributes the concluding essay in the volume. His presentation focuses on far-reaching developments in post-Cold War Asia, including shifts in the balance of power. He identifies three main trends in the region. First, Japan's movers and shakers have been preparing the country for a strategic disengagement from the United States and the recasting of priorities in favor of Asia and to some extent the United Nations. Second, China's response is to take a series of initiatives to balance Japan's power and reinforce its economic influence with overseas Chinese and non-Asian investors. Third, an obvious drift has occurred in American policy for the United States, reflecting toward military deployment inertia after the Cold War and the influence of domestic political considerations. The ultimate determination of the shift in the balance of power awaits some event or incident that will demonstrate the extent of the American preparedness for a new objective situation. The event could be set off by nuclear weapons in North Korea, the downing of an American pilot, or an action near the 38th parallel. Johnson evaluates Samuel Huntington's "Clash of Civilizations," economic integration, and social fragmentation as movements that are working themselves out in Asia. As old borders come down, new ones spring up. Fear of dominant powers and fear of being left out are twin emotions around the world. High levels of conflict threaten significant areas of the world. Johnson's unifying them is the enrichment and empowerment of Asia viewed in historical perspective.

I

CHINA, TAIWAN, AND SOUTHEAST ASIA

CHAPTER ONE

Impressions of China*

ROBERT J. MYERS

NARRATOR: We have been fortunate this year to have Dr. Robert J. Myers join the faculty of the Department of Government and Foreign Affairs at the University of Virginia. Introducing our speaker today will be Professor Shao-chuan Leng. Within the last ten years Professor Leng has built up a program in China and Asian studies that compares favorably with the best programs of any other university, and we are honored to have him introduce Professor Myers.

MR. LENG: Dr. Myers needs little introduction. He has been here before and is well known in the field. I will, however, say a few words to emphasize his accomplishments. He is a scholar, a writer, an administrator, and president of the Carnegie Council on Ethics and International Relations, where he has been able to raise millions of dollars for that organization. He was the former publisher of the *New Republic* and the co-founder and publisher of the *Washington Magazine*, with many other publications to his credit.

Having traveled widely in Asia in different capacities, Dr. Myers knows influential people in Korea, Taiwan, the PRC, and other areas. I myself was recently in China and Taiwan trying to

---

Presented in a Forum at the Miller Center of Public Affairs on 4 September 1992.

make contacts, and many people I met already knew Robert Myers. It is an honor to present Dr. Myers to you.

MR. MYERS: What I will do today is present a journalist's overview of the significant changes taking place in China. I had not been to China during the last four years, partly due to a personal pique, but mostly due to the Tiananmen Square massacre in 1989. Realizing that an absence of more than four years might undermine any claim on my part to know what is taking place in China, I accepted an invitation to go there in August to participate in an international conference sponsored by the Chinese Center for International Studies. This organization is part of the state council, an influential group similar to a governmental cabinet. As a result, I was able to meet many senior officials, including the foreign minister.

I will briefly mention three areas: Chinese politics, domestic and international; the military scene; and the Chinese economy. In the political area, the problem of succession and who will succeed Deng Xiaoping, who is now 88 years old, seems as cloudy as ever. The man usually mentioned to succeed him is General Yang Shangkun, who is 85 years old and head of the Military Council—the single most important organ of the Chinese government, and the last post Deng Xiaoping relinquished before retiring. Deng still has influence, nevertheless.

Since 1988, the central argument in China has been whether or not economic reform is possible without some concurrent liberalization of the political process. At the 13th Congress of the Communist Party in 1987, the leadership thought that concurrent economic and political reform was possible. In fact, if you are a good Communist, it is difficult to argue that economic reform can take place without having political reform at the same time.

The Chinese, however, have managed to avoid facing that doctrinal contradiction because of their lack of dedication, at least philosophically, to the Communist Party. Consequently, the same issues will come up at the 14th Congress to take place in October of this year, but the leadership will probably not pose the question of political reform.

4

I personally tried to test the waters with regard to how open the leadership was to political reform and was soundly rejected. I had written a paper for the conference entitled "Reconsidering Human Rights: East and West," which is a rather scathing attack on the Communist notions that the state controls all rights accruing to individuals and that people on their own do not have any rights whatsoever. Needless to say, they would not let me present that paper, although I did attend the conference.

The politics are difficult, and the party is still a great drag not only on politics, but the economy as well. Its membership is some 40 million strong. Because the party has many factions and is weak and divided, however, the power basically stays with the People's Liberation Army.

Deng Xiaoping resurrected himself in January of this year by going to South China, which is a booming area. He brought many leaders of the army with him to warn them against leftists. It is amazing that someone like Deng Xiaoping is worrying about leftists and rightists when all of them seem to defy political description. You can call them conservatives, but if they are reforming, how can they be conservative? In any case, Deng Xiaoping's visit to South China did seem to reinvigorate his prospects.

What China still lacks and what any dictatorship lacks is a way to have a peaceful transfer of power. Orderly succession is certainly one indicator of a country's progress toward democracy.

Internationally, the most notable recent event was the recognition of South Korea by the PRC. China's recognition is very important in settling the question of a divided Korea and in dealing with the danger posed by what appears to be North Korea's nuclear capability. China's recognition of South Korea was obviously not what the North Koreans wanted. Those present at the meeting were profoundly depressed upon hearing the foreign minister's explanation as to the value and significance of China's action, and would have preferred to have fallen through the floor. The new cooperation between China and South Korea and the resolution of the divided Korea problem will also come at considerable expense to Japan and will further complicate the Northeast Asian security situation.

The Chinese speakers at this conference were rather derisive of the Japanese. It was the first time that I had run into this attitude. They warned countries with strong economic interests not to try to convert those interests to their political and military advantage. The Chinese leaders were particularly speaking about Southeast Asia and the Association of Southeast Asian Nations (ASEAN). Frankly, what is happening in Southeast Asia, as far as American interests are concerned, distresses me.

As most of you know, our base arrangements in the Philippines have been terminated. The Russians are leaving Vietnam, and the area is being haphazardly absorbed into the Japanese trade orbit. Furthermore, over the longer term the Chinese influence will continue to become stronger as a result of propinquity.

There has been little discussion as to what the role of the United States is and should be in Southeast Asia. The Manila Conference of the ASEAN group in July was not very constructive from the point of view of the United States. Our secretary of state was there and tried to persuade the six ASEAN countries to make some kind of human rights statement about Burma, which is a total disaster by any standard in terms of the occurrence of political persecution.

The ASEAN countries normally use the same argument that China uses—that what they do with their own citizens is their own business. One had hoped that the success of the Helsinki Accords in Europe and other similar measures might lead to similar developments in Asia. Indonesia has blood on its hands as a result of the massacre of the Christians in the island of Ambon last year, and not surprisingly is speaking the same way as the Chinese with regard to human rights. Though I will not discuss human rights further today, it is a powerful tool of democratic development, and just because there are some problems, people should certainly not give up on it.

The second area I want to discuss is the military. Because I have known many of the military officers over the years, I spent a day at the Beijing Institute of Strategic Studies. In their usual amiable mood, they felt that everything was going fine. The defense budget, for example, has increased roughly 12 percent at a time when defense budgets have decreased in countries around the world. After I inquired at the Pentagon to verify those figures, I was assured that China's defense budget is $16 billion, twice what China claims. That amount, however, must be viewed in light of what the money is probably being spent on, which relates back to the question of China's political stability and legitimacy, particularly at the top levels of leadership.

Some claim that necessity has prompted the increase in the budget. For example, more money has been needed to fund troops and police to keep a lid on unrest in various parts of the country. There may be some truth to that claim. Certainly there are trends in China that might destabilize or break up the central government, and for a government that is so reliant on coercive force, spending more money to preserve itself would make a lot of sense.

There does not seem to be any particular external focus for the Chinese projection of power. With only a limited navy and air force, China has difficulty projecting their power very far. It always annoys them, however, particularly at the military level, when people refer to China as a regional power, because from their perspective, everything within the Four Seas is well within their grasp.

It is almost inevitable that the Chinese will hold sway over Southeast Asia over the next decade or two. I do not see the United States stepping into that kind of situation militarily. Beyond the Seventh Fleet bases at Yokosuka in Japan and Hawaii, the United States has access to Indonesia through the naval base at Surabaja. Other countries in the region may be marginally helpful—barnacles can be scraped in Singapore and a little help may come from Thailand—but there is little else in terms of a U.S. presence in the region.

The Southeast Asian nations also are limited in their ability to counter China's influence. Because the ASEAN countries other than Thailand have very little military capability, the idea of recreating a SEATO (Southeast Asian Treaty Organization) kind of alliance or a quasi-Asian NATO appears to be rapidly evaporating.

The third point I would like to address is China's economic development. China is, without question, the fastest-growing economy in Asia. Even in northern China where I spent a couple of weeks, there is a pace of activity that frankly surprised me. In the northwest city of Xian, there is a new airport, new highways, and several new factories.

In Jinan, a city of five million located in Shantung province near the ocean and Korea, there is also a new airport and new highways to Ch'ü-fu, which is the family grounds of Confucius and where his remains allegedly are located. With the new infrastructure and China's recent recognition of South Korea, it is very possible that there will be a great surge of building and manufacturing in provinces like Shantung, which will attract much successful investment.

In southern China, a fifth Asian tiger may be developing from Hong Kong, Taiwan, and the provinces of Guangtung (which is located next to Hong Kong), and Fujian (across from the Taiwan Straits), in which case you would have a country of 130 million people with an individual average income of $2,700, raising it above Thailand, which is considered one of the really booming countries in Southeast Asia.

Finally, I will briefly discuss the U.S. sale of 150 jet fighters (F-16s) to Taiwan. Maintaining the aerospace industry jobs, supplies, and manufacturing components is very important to the United States. In addition to yielding clear domestic benefits, the sale allows us some time to think about what our military future is likely to be.

On another level, the sale will not seriously damage our relations with mainland China. I had the opportunity to discuss that problem in Beijing, and they know that the United States will, through the Taiwan Resolution, continue to support Taiwan, which is its obligation. There are sure to be those who argue that the sale should not have been made because these jets are more technically advanced than those in previous sales. In the long term, however, the sale is a good thing for Taiwan in terms of prestige, particularly given the withdrawal of South Korea's recognition of Taiwan. What the sale might do is give Taiwan a greater feeling of security and status, which is important for them. Over time, everything will fall into place, and the arms sale will be seen as useful from the American point of view. Furthermore, the sale will not be destabilizing to Sino-American relations.

Robert J. Myers

I do not expect a qualitative rise in military capability in Taiwan and mainland China to lead to warfare. The situation has progressed beyond such a scenario taking place. The most avid investor in mainland China is now Taiwan, and it is causing the Taiwan government a great deal of trouble with regard to balance of payments and other considerations. How much money, for example, can Taiwan invest there if they are still worried about military attacks?

Ironically, arms sales to the Third World are dominated by members of the U.N. Security Council, which tries to lower such sales. The United States and China are vying for a share of that same market. With the arms sale to Taiwan, the Chinese say they will drop out of the arms negotiations and disregard their previous tacit commitment not to sell arms to the Middle East. Now they claim to be free to do that. There will certainly be some falling-out in the international sense, but by and large, the sale of the jets is good for the United States and good for Taiwan's morale. Furthermore, it will not result in any military conflict.

Politically, militarily, and economically, these are my impressions of China. I welcome your questions, and refer you now to my colleagues, Professor Leng and Professor Womack.

MR. LENG: I was in Taiwan when I first heard the announcements regarding the South Korean decision to establish normal relations with the PRC and regarding the possible U.S. sale of F-16s to Taiwan. Aside from U.S. negotiations with Beijing over what the United States might offer to prevent Beijing's violent objection to the sale, the jet deal was almost completed. Given that the Communist Chinese themselves recently bought some advanced Russian jets, are in the process of buying still more, and are even trying to build some advanced jets in cooperation with the Russians, I think that the sale of F-16s to Taiwan is a wise thing. It gives the people in Taiwan a greater sense of security, and I doubt that this would lead to any problem or any real conflict between the two sides. It will actually balance the military power of the PRC and Taiwan and allow them to continue to conduct other exchanges, while working domestically to U.S. advantage also.

9

MR. WOMACK: Relating to an area of my special interest, which is China's relations with Southeast Asia, I would agree that China is going to play an increasing role in the region, especially since there is no real countervailing strategic force to the kind of influence that China can have. Southeast Asia has a population that is a little larger than that of Latin America, and the many growing economies there make Southeast Asia an important area.

The military dynamics of the region do not bother me much. What is troubling, however, is the loss of U.S. political and economic presence in the region. This may stem simply from our ignorance of the region, a lack of engagement, or a feeling that with the end of the Vietnam War, a policy of benign distance from most countries (or malevolent distance in the case of Vietnam) is acceptable. There is no crisis, so the United States does not need to rethink its policy.

If these serious problems are not addressed, people will come to regret it in the 1990s as developments continue in Southeast Asia.

QUESTION: Some have said that the question is not when the PRC will take over Hong Kong, but when the entrepreneurial spirit of Hong Kong will take over the PRC. Do you have any comments?

MR. MYERS: A book that came out five or six years ago called *How the West Got Rich* listed several rather mundane elements contributing to the success of the West, like double-entry bookkeeping, reliable banking, and insurance. The main factor was a kind of Martin Luther notion about there having to be a psychological belief system that made it possible for people to pursue wealth as a legitimate goal of the society. This will be an obstacle in China, as it is in Russia and the other republics, because the Communist leaders of China have stridently insisted for so long that making money is bad and that social concerns, the safety nets, and the iron rice bowl are more important.

I remember when McDonald's opened their store a few years ago in Taiwan and three months later announced that it was the most profitable one in the whole chain. A number of Taiwanese immediately organized a consumer group and forced McDonald's to lower the price by over 25 percent. This action was significant because Taiwan is not noted for such ideas.

In Beijing I talked to the head of one of the major fast food chains, Pepsico, which encountered the same situation. They had opened a Kentucky Fried Chicken restaurant, and within three months it was the most profitable one in their chain. With half the ownership being government officials, they thought it would be a great idea to publicly propose a big dividend. I recounted to him the Taiwan experience and said that such an announcement would not go over well, particularly in China. I suggested that he just pay the dividend quietly and worry about promoting capitalism on a sunnier day.

Because of Hong Kong and Western influences, the attitudes of the people in southern China are more favorable toward the capitalistic system. The people in Guangtung province and Fujian, for example, are a little exceptional in that they have long been noted for their entrepreneurial character. Most of the overseas Chinese originated in these provinces; they leave home to make money and have this "let's get out there and do it" attitude.

In other parts of China, there certainly are new opportunities to make money. At one stage, Deng Xiaoping said that getting rich is now acceptable, but still, that attitude will need time to take hold. Also, if the entrepreneurs are too aggressive, they will find themselves slipping backwards again. Perhaps over time—maybe 50 years—China will have much more of a capitalist society. The great thing that they did under Zhao Ziyang, the former head of the party who is now under house arrest, was to open agriculture so that people could own their own land, keep a high percentage of their crops, and not have to sell everything to the government. That change in rural policy affected about 80 percent of the population. The Russians attempted a similar policy but failed, because in their collectivist economy, less than 15 percent of their population would have been affected by agricultural reforms.

China has built this system very intelligently. A little over half of the industry and business in China is private. State-run operations, which are usually financial disasters, are being closed down and reintegrated.

You are correct in saying that Hong Kong is an analogue for Western capitalism, but it will have some obstacles to overcome because of history.

QUESTION: In contemplating the prospective arrival of democracy in China, do you think we would also have to consider the simultaneous secession of provinces, ethnic wars, or territorial disorder with the total loss of strong, central control?

MR. LENG: China is quite different from the Soviet Union. There are minority groups, but they are much smaller in number. There is also a strong sense of Chinese nationalism. Even though regionally people may try to seek more autonomy from the central government, disintegration is something to which few Chinese will subscribe.

When we make comparative studies of the former Soviet Union and China, another factor unique to China's development is the overseas Chinese. That is the single most important factor in the Chinese economy. The overseas Chinese invest many millions of dollars in China, particularly in Beijing, Guangzhou, and Fujian. The overseas Chinese have opened the biggest McDonald's in the world in Beijing. I tried to go there to try it, but the line was much too long, so I never did.

Circumstances in China are changing quickly, particularly in the economic area. The economy and economists in China will be a very important part of the inevitable political changes in the future.

QUESTION: The most-favored-nation (MFN) trading agreement recently renewed with China has favorable economic results as far as the United States is concerned. Would the threatened termination of the MFN clause put any additional political pressure on the Chinese with respect to human rights?

MR. MYERS: The use of economic sanctions, quotas, and similar measures have almost never been an effective political lever, because these measures tend to cut both ways. (The case of South Africa is a possible exception, and even that is questionable.) The effect of MFN pressures on China will probably be minimal, now that it is getting so much stronger economically. There are all kinds of ways to avoid those restrictions if people are so disposed. Basically, the human rights problem is probably beyond our direct intervention.

Chinese tradition, at least with regard to the imperial system, allows for substantially more political change than the communist one does. On the other hand, China is such a big country, with almost 25 percent of the world's population. There is the possibility that the Chinese example will be seen as a new kind of authoritarian approach to the problems of the world, but not many people want to emulate it. If we are to improve the human rights situation in China and support the age-old hope that China will evolve to a more open political system with democratic values that are certainly not unpopular in China, much patience will be required.

QUESTION: I have been told that in 1949 Hong Kong was colonized by Shanghai businessmen fleeing the Communist takeover and that the Shanghai entrepreneurial spirit was responsible for Hong Kong's success. Have you seen any evidence of Shanghai reasserting itself as a leader of world trade and contact with the West?

MR. MYERS: There has been a significant policy change in Beijing, and they are now trying to develop the Shanghai area, which inevitably will become the most significant commercial center, because it is located in the Yangtze basin. The area is likely to re-attract banking, insurance, and other kinds of financial services that Hong Kong has. Some Shanghai businessmen and some Taiwanese visiting Shanghai said that Shanghai was the only place in Asia growing so fast that a person could make substantial amounts of money even after sharing 50 percent with the officials.

QUESTION: With regard to the situation in Southeast Asia, the reconciliation between China and South Korea, and their relationship with the ASEAN nations, how will these changes affect Japan? They are major suppliers for Japanese industry and a strong market for Japanese goods.

MR. MYERS: Japan has dominated most of the economies and most of the investment in the region. They do not absorb many products from Southeast Asia. In the three-way competition between China, Japan, and the United States, the United States seems to be lagging. Over the next 20 to 30 years, the United States will more likely concentrate on the North American Free Trade Agreement and how it is going to come to grips with Asian competition.

The EC might also come apart. While a year or so ago there was much more momentum behind the Uruguay Round or at least larger trade zones, the recession or depression—depending on one's perspective—has certainly altered many business patterns. For example, I met a successful Taiwanese businessman who manufactures Puma tennis shoes, but he cannot manufacture them in Taiwan. He cannot manufacture them in Korea, either, which forces his base of operations to change rapidly. Some companies, like Motorola for example, obviously have had great successes in a tough field, but whether the United States will be able to play that game remains uncertain.

During my visit earlier this year, China struck me as being a vibrant place. Having first visited some of the same places in China in 1945, it is astounding what they are doing. The basic infrastructure is being built, and there is an enormous number of people—something like 1.2 billion—who all look good, alert, and work hard. In the villages you can buy zhao-zi (little dumplings) from street vendors, among other things. The morale seems good and the expectations of the people seem high. What is happening in China may be good for both China and the world, but the United States needs to do some rethinking and introspection if it is to participate in what is taking place in the region.

MR. WOMACK: The primary dimension of the competition between China and Japan in Southeast Asia is going to be economic, and economic competition is not as exclusive. It is also far more complex than military competition. Japan can invest in a country like Vietnam, as Vietnam is now opening up to foreign investment, but Thailand, South Korea, Taiwan, and Europe can invest there as well.

14

Some of the U.S. oil companies are certainly covering their openings into the market, but this is still a weak area for the United States as a whole. It is an area that demands a much finer sense of opportunities than in previous times when the United States would become involved in a country so as to oppose the Russians. Now the question is, can a U.S. company make money and develop a share of the market in this area? There will be a different kind of challenge to the American role in the future, and hopefully the United States can meet that challenge in a place like Southeast Asia. Eventually it also affects strategic and military concerns.

QUESTION: Professor Womack, what advantages are there for the United States to reconcile its differences with Hanoi?

MR. WOMACK: Changing U.S. policy toward Vietnam is long overdue. Forward-looking arguments from politicians or diplomats in favor of the continued nonrecognition of Vietnam are rare. Refusing to recognize Vietnam has cost the United States a lot. The cost has not been obvious, but much sand has slid through the hourglass and much opportunity has been lost in the last 10 to 15 years. The policy toward Southeast Asia should be readjusted to suit changing needs and circumstances.

QUESTION: Is the increase in the military portion of China's budget related to employment issues as it is in some other countries right now? When I was in India about a month and a half ago, I sensed that there was increasing concern regarding their borders with China. It strikes me that the increases in military expenditures are so great that the initial explanation for it is not very persuasive. Do you have more information on the breakdown of that increase? How much is it in personnel versus hardware?

MR. MYERS: The Pentagon looks upon the increase as very threatening. The Chinese, the Indians, and others are buying up sophisticated Russian equipment. China's submarine fleet is now up to roughly 100 and it may have one nuclear submarine. China has the capability to refuel jets in midair, which means its forces can be projected considerably further. China is the only Asian country that possesses atomic weapons. From the Pentagon perspective, this development is rather threatening.

If you talk to the Chinese staff generals, however, they claim that most of this money will be spent for long-overdue pay raises and better treatment of the troops. On the other hand, half-hour television programs show heroic events of the Chinese military every night, and that to some would look rather militaristic. Furthermore, in terms of the strategic situation in the Asian-Pacific region, particularly Southeast Asia, time is on the Chinese side to have their traditional role asserted again.

China is an example of a country that for a couple of hundred years dropped out of the international community—not of its own volition, but because of circumstances. They were not able to play the heavy role in their part of the world as they had done for centuries. The Chinese explanation for it is based on their cyclical idea of history that sometimes the country performs well and sometimes it does not. We in the United States may have to rethink our notion that we are part of a steady linear progress in history.

I really do not think a $16 billion military budget for a country the size of China is that important. Most of that money must go toward maintaining the troops and their hardware, which costs money even in China. I do not see China's increased military budget as incremental aggression at all.

NARRATOR: I would like to thank Professors Leng and Womack for their contribution to today's presentation. We would especially like to thank Professor Myers for sharing with us his knowledgeable impressions of China.

CHAPTER TWO

China and Taiwan*

SHAO-CHUAN LENG

NARRATOR: Professor Leng has been both a tower of strength for the Miller Center and a mainstay of the Department of Government and Foreign Affairs at the University of Virginia. For many years, he has taught full-time in the department, even when he enjoyed a research assignment. He was born in Chengtu, China, in 1921 and has been a naturalized U.S. citizen since 1953. He received a master's degree in international relations from Yale University in 1948 and a doctorate in political science from the University of Pennsylvania in 1950.

Professor Leng has helped the Miller Center establish the foreign affairs and Asian side of its program and has also assisted in the development of a Chinese political leadership program at the Miller Center. He has edited a Miller Center book series on Asian political leadership. In addition, Professor Leng has written and edited other books and published many articles. The Miller Center will always be grateful for his leadership and are honored that he has agreed to discuss relations between China and Taiwan.

MR. LENG: I will begin my discussion with a brief historical survey of Taiwan's relations with mainland China. Taiwan was once part of China but was ceded to Japan in 1895 following the Sino-

---

Presented in a Forum at the Miller Center of Public Affairs on 11 April 1996.

Japanese War. Japan ruled Taiwan as a colony for 50 years, until the Chinese Nationalist (Kuomintang) government reclaimed Taiwan from the Japanese in 1945. Initially, the Taiwanese enthusiastically welcomed the arrival of the mainlanders. Unfortunately, the man sent by Chiang Kai-shek to reclaim Taiwan, Chen Yi, was an inept, corrupt governor who did much to damage the Kuomintang (KMT) government's reputation. As a result of his ineptness and corruption, much tension arose between the Taiwanese and the mainlanders, which led to widespread riots and uprisings that were ruthlessly suppressed by Nationalist forces. In short, it was not a very happy beginning.

After losing the civil war on the mainland to the Chinese Communists in 1949, Chiang Kai-shek retreated with his followers to Taiwan. To support his continuing fight against the Chinese Communists, he transplanted his one-party government from mainland China to Taiwan and declared martial law on the island. Chiang's government on Taiwan was dominated by mainlanders with only a few token posts left for the native Taiwanese.

The KMT government, however, did provide a politically stable environment that was necessary for economic development. This factor, along with a number of others, contributed to Taiwan's economic transformation. Among these other factors was the support of U.S. technical and economic aid, which ended in 1960 due to Taiwan's success. The sound development strategy of government-adopted reform and the presence of entrepreneurs, technocrats, and well-trained, skilled labor forces contributed to Taiwan's economic transformation, later known as Taiwan's "economic miracle." Taiwan's increased GNP is but one indicator of Taiwan's progress. From 1953 to 1988, Taiwan's GNP grew at an annual rate of almost 9 percent, which is tremendous. In 1950 its per capita GNP was about $150. In 1988 it was over $6,000, and this trend has continued. The per capita GNP of Taiwan today is approximately $12,000, a very impressive gain.

With economic development came gradual political liberalization. Chiang Kai-shek died in 1975, and his successors began actively recruiting Taiwanese into the government and the KMT Party. Chiang Ching-kuo—Chiang Kai-shek's son who later became president of Taiwan—decided to make some important moves toward political liberalization in the 1980s. In 1986 he allowed an opposition party called the Democratic Progressive Party (DPP) to be established for the first time. In 1987 Chiang Ching-kuo lifted martial law and allowed Taiwan's residents to visit relatives on mainland China. His actions laid the foundation for the so-called process of Taiwanization and democratization. When Chiang Ching-kuo died in 1988, Taiwanese Vice President Lee Teng-hui became president of Taiwan and also chairman of the KMT. Lee has continued what Chiang Ching-kuo began and has vigorously pushed for the continued democratization and Taiwanization of the party and the government.

These efforts greatly enhanced not only the protection of human rights, but also the protection of freedom of speech and press in Taiwan. The most telling evidence of democratization, though, has been Taiwan's elections since 1991. Though there is no question that the KMT ruling party has enjoyed some special advantages—such as funding and television networks—these elections, including the recent presidential, legislative, gubernatorial, and mayoral elections, have nonetheless been generally praised by outside observers as free, open, and fair. In fact, the level of Taiwan's achievements is comparable to Japan's achievements.

What are Taiwan's problems? Are there serious, ethnic conflicts in Taiwan? A recent issue of *Foreign Affairs* includes a sponsored statement by Taiwan's premier and newly elected vice president, Dr. Lien Chan, which addresses this issue. In his statement, Lien observes that nearly all Taiwanese can trace their ancestry to the Chinese mainland. In other words, those on the mainland and those on the island are all Chinese. He is right: Of the 21 million people in Taiwan, 84 percent are the so-called Taiwanese, the early Chinese who went to Taiwan. Of the remaining population, 14 percent are mainlanders, who are the newcomers, and 2 percent are aborigines. In short, cultural ethnic differences are few; there are more differences between the mainland and Taiwan in the area of politics.

Taiwan's current political parties are organized along subethnic lines. For example, the opposition party, or the DPP, is essentially a Taiwanese party with its strength in the south. The DPP seeks independence for Taiwan. The second party is the New Party, which is primarily supported by mainlanders, mostly from the Taipei area. The New Party stands for eventual unification and better relations with the mainland. The KMT is positioned between these two parties in the political spectrum and draws support from both mainlanders and Taiwanese. It is committed theoretically to a "one China" policy. In practice, however, its approach to Taiwan-China relations is more a gradual stage-by-stage process toward establishing Taiwan as an independent political entity. The differences between the political parties reflect the political division that exists among the population as a whole, particularly over the sensitive issue of unification versus independence. Last year public opinion surveys conducted by the two largest newspapers in Taiwan found 20 percent of the population in favor of independence and about 22 percent in favor of unification. The majority, or about 50 percent, supported maintaining the status quo.

The recent presidential election reflected this division. Lee Teng-hui won because his position, which was not to push for either independence or unification, was the same as that of the majority— though it is true that Beijing's missile-testing before the election helped Lee gain more votes. Beijing does not have the common sense to behave, and they therefore hurt their own cause. The same thing happened in the late 1950s, when the Japan Socialist Party (JSP) was running a campaign against Japan's ruling party, the Liberal Democratic Party (LDP). The Chinese Communists came out openly in support of the JSP, and as a result, the JSP suffered a stunning defeat. Forty years later, Beijing still has not learned its lesson.

In relation to Beijing's and Taipei's policies, since assuming power Deng Xiaoping has abandoned Mao Zedong's policy, which favored the liberation of Taiwan by force. In its place Deng adopted the policy of the peaceful unification of China. In 1979 and 1981 the PRC offered to hold talks with Taipei and tried to offer what it considered acceptable terms for future unification. Beijing assured Taiwan that after unification, Taiwan would enjoy a high degree of autonomy and would be able to retain its armed forces, socioeconomic system, and way of life. In the 1980s Deng Xiaoping further elaborated on this position by describing it as "one country, two systems." He said that under this policy, socialism in

China and capitalism in Taiwan could coexist and develop side by side for many years after unification.

Chiang Ching-kuo would have nothing to do with the Communists while he was alive, even though he did lift martial law and allow the Taiwanese to visit mainland China. When Mr. Lee became president in 1990, he made a very important speech on the subject. He said that mainland China and Taiwan were both indivisible parts of China and that all Chinese should seek peaceful, democratic means to achieve unification; however, he also asked the PRC to recognize Taiwan as a political entity and to renounce the use of force. In short, Taipei and Beijing take two different stands on the issue or reunification. Beijing stands for "one country, two systems," while Taipei stands for one country, two political entities. In 1991, however, Taipei established a National Unification Council that proposed guidelines for unification through a three-stage process with no fixed timetable.

In the meantime, quasi-organizations—both semi-official and private—have been formed in both Beijing and Taipei. In Taiwan it is called the Straits Exchange Foundation, and the one in Beijing was named the Association for Relations Across the Taiwan Straits. Both were established in 1990-1991 to handle bilateral relations between the PRC and Taiwan. In meetings between the heads of the two semi-official organizations they have been able to institute the framework for increasing contacts and for developing regular channels of communication between the two sides.

During this period, economic exchange has expanded enormously between mainland China and Taiwan. Trade between them, via Hong Kong, reached $17 billion in 1994. Despite the current crisis, trade continues to increase. Taiwan has a $14 billion trade surplus with mainland China and its investment on the mainland is around $24 billion. Economically, therefore, interdependence between the two sides is increasing, but there still has been no political breakthrough. In the first half of last year, a gradual progression toward direct talks between the two sides seemed to be taking place. Jiang Zemin, president of the PRC, offered an eight-point proposal in early 1995, to which Lee Teng-hui of Taipei responded with a six-point proposal. Even though they never gave up their stands, the tone of the statements was conciliatory and

21

flexible, increasing people's hopes for better relations. President Lee's visit to the United States in June 1995, however, severely strained mainland-Taiwan relations and hindered further progress.

Taiwan now has diplomatic relations with only about 30 countries. Moreover, except for the Vatican and South Africa, most of the states that officially recognize Taiwan are small states. On the other hand, Taiwan has developed cultural and unofficial ties with many countries. Since its economy is doing so well now—with its per capita GNP of $12,000 and a foreign reserve exchange of $100 million—Taiwan feels it can be more assertive in enhancing its international role, pressing for membership to international organizations, and developing its official ties with more foreign countries. Since 1993 it has even tried to enter the United Nations, albeit unsuccessfully. Mr. Lee's visit to Cornell in June 1995 was designed as a media event and is another example of Taipei's increased assertiveness. Beijing, however, viewed his trip as a dangerous attempt to seek international recognition of Taiwan's independence. Consequently, the PRC reacted violently by recalling its ambassadors to the United States and breaking scheduled talks with the U.S. government. As a warning to Taiwan, Beijing also staged a series of missile tests in July and August in the East China Sea, which further strained relations. Semi-official talks between Taipei and Beijing stopped. Fortunately, the crisis is now over, and relations can be expected to revert back to the way they were before Lee's visit to the United States. It is hoped that the dialogue will continue and will eventually lead to the development of direct links between the two sides because creating a mutual trust is the best way to handle this situation.

QUESTION: Will Beijing's relations with Hong Kong influence relations between Beijing and Taipei in the coming years?

MR. LENG: The PRC's handling of Hong Kong will definitely affect its relations with Taiwan. Hong Kong will be returned to China in 1997, which means that Taipei will have to develop direct trade with China because Hong Kong will no longer be available as an independent intermediary of trade. Furthermore, if the PRC hopes to influence the Taiwanese, it must keep its promise to Hong

Kong to uphold the idea of "one country, two systems" by respecting Hong Kong's autonomy in economic and social fields. Otherwise, the people of Taiwan will be even further alienated.

COMMENT: The Chinese mainland has the largest standing army in the world, and the United States has helped the Taiwanese government to develop a reputable and well-equipped military. In light of these facts, it is hard for me to see how Beijing and Taipei, which have been in conflict for so long, are ever going to become one entity.

MR. LENG: The current state of Beijing-Taipei relations could last forever. There is no timetable. The important thing is to defuse tensions on both sides because a war or an armed conflict would not be in the interests of either party. China will probably never sanction an invasion, but it might still fire missiles at Taiwan, which would seriously damage both the Taiwanese economy and the psychology of its people. Moreover, Taiwan would most likely respond to China's actions, and the United States could not stand by if it did. Hence, any armed conflict will be a loss for everyone. A win-win situation for all of the participants involved would require a resumption of talks between Taiwan and Beijing and an arrangement of peaceful coexistence that would foster the development of mutual trust, something that is totally missing from the current situation.

QUESTION: How consistent has U.S. foreign policy been toward China and Taiwan in recent years and what should U.S. policy be in the future?

MR. LENG: The United States has a one-China policy; that is, the United States recognizes the PRC as the government of China and does not recognize Taiwan as a separate political entity. At the same time, however, the three Sino-American communiques plus the Taiwan Relations Act all reflect the U.S. desire to see that the issue of Taiwan is resolved peacefully. U.S. policy is currently aimed at balancing its commitment to a one-China policy with its obligation to keep the Taiwan Strait peaceful and stable. The

United States has important interests in stability and peace in the Asian-Pacific region. While not wanting to encourage Taiwan's independence, the United States wants to see the peaceful resolution of disputes. In this sense, the recent crisis may have a positive side. It clarified the limits for all parties involved. China, for example, made clear how seriously it viewed any attempts by Taiwan to gain independence and that it was willing to use force if necessary to prevent that possibility. I hope the recent confrontation will teach all parties concerned to exercise self-restraint and be less provocative.

QUESTION: Is there a generational change taking place in China?

MR. LENG: Yes, many changes are taking place in the PRC. China is currently developing economically, but it still needs to politically liberalize. I hope that political liberalization will follow its economic reforms, as was the gradual outcome in both South Korea and Taiwan. Visitors to China often observe a number of contradictions. For example, corruption and capitalism exist side by side with Communist Party control. To retain its privileged position in power, the Chinese Communist Party has continued to support "communism," although the ideology is now bankrupt. I doubt if even 50 party members currently believe in communism; they now worship making money.

QUESTION: What about China's succession crisis?

MR. LENG: This is a recurrent problem. Elections and succession crises unfortunately encourage hard-line positions, and this has been a difficult year, since it is an election year in both the United States and Taiwan as well as a transitional period for Beijing. As a result, no leader can afford to be too soft toward the other side. Domestic politics have had a great influence on the external postures of all of the parties concerned.

QUESTION: It strikes me that President Lee is the key man in this situation. With 54 percent of the vote, he has a large mandate. What kind of person is he? Is he a reasonable person? Is he a person who can negotiate differences, or does he tend to be an ideologue or even an opportunist?

MR. LENG: President Lee is an unpredictable person, and he does appear to have a missionary zeal. He has strong views, and I do not know how much advice he is willing to take from others. On the other hand, he is well educated and has good intentions. Judging from what he did to consolidate his power after Chiang Ching-kuo's death, he is also a skillful politician. He is realistic enough to know what can and what cannot be done. Hence, he will probably not push too far, even after his overwhelming victory.

QUESTION: Would you agree that Beijing's handling of the coming reunification with Hong Kong and its stated "one China, two systems" provide Taiwan with an ideal opportunity to test the sincerity of the Chinese pledge, and that if Beijing handles Hong Kong as promised, Taiwan would be persuaded to be more forthcoming in the future regarding unification?

MR. LENG: Yes, I am in total agreement. Thanks to the existence of the *de facto* autonomy of Taiwan, Hong Kong will probably receive better treatment from China. Beijing is very conscious of the fact that the world is watching. It knows that it had better keep its promise to Hong Kong or risk further alienating the people on Taiwan.

QUESTION: Why is mainland China so obsessed with the idea of unification?

MR. LENG: Ezra Vogel, the well-known scholar and expert on Chinese affairs at Harvard and a consultant to the U.S. government, recently commented on this issue. He said that Chinese leaders regard Taiwan as part of China in much the same way that President Lincoln regarded the South as part of the United States. Perhaps the leadership and attitudes will change in the long run, but if my recent trip to China is any indication, attitudes toward Taiwan are unlikely to change in the near future. My discussions with intellectuals, students, and businessmen indicated that Chinese nationalism appears to be gaining strength due to the ideological vacuum in China. Some people were quite critical of the PRC's domestic policy and even its treatment of Taiwan, but only a small percentage of the people I encountered felt that Taiwan was not part of China. Moreover, they are willing to wait. It is necessary for people to understand that the issue of Taiwan is a sensitive and emotional one and the less one talks about it the better. Given the political and economic gap between the two sides, it is not realistic to talk about unification.

QUESTION: Is China, by tradition and history, a hegemonic imperial power?

MR. LENG: For the time being, China is not an expansionist state, even though the media in the United States often talks about containing China. Moreover, China considers the Taiwan question to be a domestic, internal matter, not an external one. By contrast, the leaders in Taiwan are trying to internationalize the issue. All that the United States can do is to develop a new system that allows Taiwan to join international organizations without being an independent state or special region. International law should grow in accordance with the changing environment. Taiwan deserves its due because of its political democratization and economic development.

QUESTION: Beijing's policy toward the United States appears to be very successful on almost every contested issue, including Taiwan and trade. Moreover, it seems to be succeeding by making promises that it does not keep. Is Beijing's foreign office that good, or is the U.S. foreign office that bad?

MR. LENG: Sometimes it is hard to understand why the PRC has behaved the way it has, particularly with respect to sensitive issues such as missile testing, arms sales, and international property rights. The best way to respond to Beijing is to enforce target sanctions on a case-by-case basis instead of grouping everything together. The fact that the PRC is currently undergoing a process of uncertain succession should also be considered; sometimes the right hand does not know what the left is doing. Again, responding to Beijing on a case-by-case basis would be more productive.

NARRATOR: Thank you, Professor Leng, for sharing your wisdom and extensive knowledge of relations between China and Taiwan.

CHAPTER THREE

China and Southeast Asia after the Cold War[*]

BRANTLY WOMACK

MR. SHAO-CHUAN LENG: Our speaker, Professor Brantly Womack, teaches Chinese politics at the University of Virginia and is associated with the Miller Center. He received his Ph.D. from the University of Chicago and has taught at both Northern Illinois University and the University of London. He has published widely on Chinese foreign policy and Southeast Asia, including Vietnam. He has recently returned from a two-week stay in Vietnam, so he is definitely an authority in this field.

MR. WOMACK: My analysis of China and Southeast Asia will be general. This is unfortunate, because the details of China's relations with Southeast Asia are endlessly fascinating. I could easily concentrate on China's relations with Singapore or Burma. I could assess the complex relationship between China, the ethnic Chinese of Southeast Asia, and the indigenous economies of Southeast Asia—all of which are autonomous actors. I could spend the next semester appraising the relationship between Vietnam and China and the complexities that have defined Vietnam as a political entity over the last 2,000 years. A discussion of the Sino-

---

[*]*Presented in a Forum at the Miller Center of Public Affairs on 16 November 1992.*

Vietnamese relation is especially tempting, because it will certainly be an important area—perhaps the key area—for problems at least in the relationship between China and Southeast Asia in the 1990s and beyond.

In this discussion, I shall deal in generalities. The generalities that I will describe are, first, the overall pattern of development of relations between China and Southeast Asia and second, the relative positions of China and Southeast Asia—how China looks to Southeast Asia and how Southeast Asia looks to China. Finally, I will explore possible problems in their relationship and the implications for U.S. foreign policy.

I

Regarding the general pattern of development, the 1950s pattern was very different from the current one. In the 1950s, Vietnam was China's socialist ally in the region. Burma, Indonesia, and eventually Cambodia under Sihanouk were China's neutral friends in the region. The other countries were not necessarily personal enemies of China, but their alliances or relations with foreign powers in the Cold War meant that their relations were hostile. In the 1960s, the relationships of China to Southeast Asia polarized, and Vietnam became China's wartime ally, grudgingly shared with the Soviet Union.

China's Cultural Revolution increased Chinese support for insurrectionary movements in other countries, and greater demands on countries of the region weakened neutralist ties and friendships. Most importantly in 1965, the coup and countercoup in Indonesia led to a breaking of the Sino-Indonesian relationship. By 1967 China and Indonesia had downgraded their relationship from the ambassadorial level. Relations between China and Indonesia were not restored until the end of 1990, as a result of the polarizing pattern set in the 1960s.

In China's relations with Vietnam, the 1970s saw a change in the Cold War pattern. As Sino-American relations improved and permitted normalization of relations in the 1970s, most of the Southeast Asian countries, with the exception of Singapore and

Indonesia, normalized their relations with China. The relationships, however, did not develop into friendships, and these countries were still worried about the continuing Chinese support for Communist parties in their countries. The most interesting development was what happened to Sino-Vietnamese relations after the Vietnamese victory and reunification. Contrary to expectations that the Vietnamese victory would build up the Communist bloc and add to the domino momentum, which had been the core of U.S. strategic policy and involvement in the war, hostility developed between China and Vietnam.

The origins of that hostility are complicated, and include three major components. First, both Vietnam and China had unrealistic expectations of what victory would mean for them. Second, after the war, Vietnam was put in a position of having to choose between its alliance with the Soviet Union and its alliance with China. Because it was richer and more distant, the Soviet Union was the more attractive choice. Incidentally, China was closely involved in forcing Vietnam's choice in that situation, compounded by Vietnam's willingness to choose due to its fear of China.

Lastly, the alliance that developed in the late 1970s between the Khmer Rouge and the Chinese, in which the Chinese in 1978 were supplying military equipment to the Khmer Rouge in Cambodia as fast as they could, led to the Vietnamese invasion of Cambodia, the Chinese invasion of Vietnam in 1979, and the definition of a hostile relationship between the two countries that persisted for most of the 1980s. The 1980s, therefore, were redefined by the unexpected and late development of this hostile relationship between China and Vietnam. The hostility between China and Vietnam allowed China to transform its relations with Southeast Asia by forming an alliance between ASEAN and the United States against Vietnam to isolate Vietnam for its policies in Cambodia.

China's alliance with most of the countries of Southeast Asia provided an umbrella for a vast expansion of economic and diplomatic links between China and Southeast Asia and eventually even military links between Burma, Thailand, and China. Basically, China was able to redefine its economic and diplomatic ties in the context of a shared enemy. By the end of the 1980s, however,

Southeast Asian countries were no longer treating Vietnam as a threat, but as a market, and China's continued hostility in support for the Khmer Rouge was eroding China's capacity to keep up with the new situation in Southeast Asia. With the development of a different policy on Vietnam's part, especially the unilateral withdrawal of Vietnamese troops from Cambodia in 1989, the stage was set for a new phase in the relationship.

As for the 1990s, the end of the Cold War and the end of the Vietnamese occupation of Cambodia have meant that there is no Soviet threat in Southeast Asia—no Soviet threat for China on which to found its own anti-Vietnamese policy. This situation combined with the simultaneous withdrawal of the United States from the Philippines has created a situation that might be described as Asia for Asians. The primary actors in Asia are now the Asian countries themselves, and this is particularly true for Southeast Asia.

This region continues to experience economic growth and bases its foreign relations primarily on economics rather than military alliances or strategic thinking. This characteristic of Southeast Asia as a region is responsible for its rather low profile in world news. It is not a crisis situation; it is a situation of economic progress.

Continued economic growth, however, shifts relationships. Uneven development creates new opportunities. No country is growing faster than China, and no region is growing faster than Southeast Asia. Because of the region's growth, its prospects for the 1990s must be looked at carefully, even in a noncrisis situation.

II

What do these two places mean for each other? What does Southeast Asia mean for China in the 1990s, and what does China mean to Southeast Asia?

For China, Southeast Asia in the 1990s has a new importance. First of all, the 1989 Tiananmen Square incident, followed by world reaction to this crisis and the end of the Cold War, required China to reassess its relationship with the rest of Asia. Even though Asia was important for China before, China viewed itself as a global actor. Now in the 1990s, China is recognizing its role and capacity as a regional actor. Its global mentality has been shaken. China appreciated the relative support from Asian countries that it received after the Tiananmen Square incident, especially in comparison to the reaction from Europe and the United States. In addition, the changes in Vietnam's policies toward Cambodia and the declining popularity of China's support for the Khmer Rouge meant that the continuing basis of China's alliances in Southeast Asia was deteriorating and that it had to rethink its particular policies in that region.

China's new policy will be created on the basis of the economic importance of Southeast Asia. Here is a region with a population equal to all of Latin America. China's trade with Southeast Asia, as a percentage of Japanese trade, was 37 percent in 1989 and 42 percent in 1990. Its exports to Southeast Asia are 44 percent of its exports to Japan. Economically, Southeast Asia in the 1990s is moving from a position of being one-third as important as Japan is to China, to being half as important as Japan is to China—and Japan is the single most important economic factor for China. Southeast Asia, therefore, is a significant region, even though China does not consider its regional relation with Southeast Asia as a dominant concern.

From a domestic perspective, China's trade with Southeast Asia was 56 percent of its trade with the United States in 1989 and 59 percent of its trade with the United States in 1990, and its exports to Southeast Asia in 1990 were 76 percent of its exports to the United States. What this means is that in the course of the 1990s, probably by 1995, China's exports to Southeast Asia may be at the same level as its exports to the United States, especially if the United States acts to control its imbalance of trade with China. Also, China's exports to Southeast Asia are far more solidly based than its exports to the United States. Thus, when the presidential candidates in the first debate in 1992 talked about the dangers of isolating China, it was somewhat similar to the old headline in the London *Times* about fog in the Channel isolating the continent. The question is whether the United States will isolate itself by making moves that no longer correspond to the capacity of the United States in economic terms.

Besides Southeast Asia's given economic importance to China, it is also significant as a frontier for China's expanding influence. As China redefines and asserts itself, it will see Southeast Asia as an area of ambiguity and apparent opportunity. This outlook will present both opportunities and threats for Southeast Asia.

What does China look like to Southeast Asia? In contrast to how the United States views China, Southeast Asia sees China as very close and very big. In general, Americans do not have much sense of the magnitude of the Chinese economy. We think of it as a poor country that exports potholders and various things that we find at discount stores. We do not think of the magnitude of the economy itself.

Let's consider the world ranking in productivity for some of China's major industrial goods. The 1991 *Chinese Statistical Abstract* lists China as fourth in steel production, first in coal, sixth in petroleum production, fourth in electricity, first in cement, third in sulfuric acid, third in chemical fertilizer, sixth in synthetic rubber, and tenth in automobiles. Figures for 1989 show that China was eighth in shipbuilding, fourth in chemical synthetic fibers, first in cotton, fourth in woven goods, sixth in sugar, and first in the production of television sets. The last number mentioned is probably helped by the fact that China may be the only country still producing black and white television sets.

The Southeast Asian perspective is very different from an American perspective. Of the above categories, Indonesia ranks tenth in chemical fertilizer, and Thailand ranks eighth in sugar production. Those are the only two Southeast Asian countries on any of these lists. For Southeast Asia, therefore, China is a major economic mass that creates a strong gravitational pull on the region, and this mass is increasing by 6 to 14 percent a year. Regardless of trade availability, this is a gravitational fact, and while China's economic growth creates vast opportunities for Southeast Asian countries, it also creates concerns about being too close to such a large country.

If we look at this issue in military terms, China's strategic nuclear forces in 1991 included only eight intercontinental ballistic missiles, 60 regional ballistic missiles, only one missile submarine (and it is always in port with problems), and 44 tactical submarines, including only five nuclear submarines. China's military expenses are estimated at $11-$22 billion, which by U.S. standards is fairly trivial. The United States has a total of about 1,500 intercontinental ballistic missiles, including Navy supplies. It has approximately 110 submarines, including 25 strategic submarines, 87 tactical submarines, and a defense budget in 1991 of $287 billion.

By U.S. standards and those of the Cold War, China, while not trivial, is not in the same league as the United States and the former Soviet Union, now Russia. By Southeast Asian standards, however, these statistics look very different. Taking Indonesia for the purpose of comparison, Indonesia has no missiles, two submarines, and a defense expenditure of $1.6 billion—which is one-tenth of China's—and Indonesia, with a relatively developed military, is the largest of the countries in Southeast Asia.

The Southeast Asian countries have no hope of military parity with China; whatever level of threat posed by China is a level of threat that is well beyond the capacity of any Southeast Asian country acting individually. Furthermore, there is no tradition and no effective institutions of regional action vis-à-vis China. China, however, is not the only Asian country in the Pacific. Consider Japan, for example. Though Japan has no nuclear arsenal, it does have 17 submarines and a larger navy than China's. Japan's military budget is $34 billion, meaning it is half again the largest estimate of Chinese defense expenditures and perhaps three times China's actual level. Clearly, Japan is still a major actor, but do Indonesia, Vietnam, or the Philippines breathe more easily because Japan is there? That is a good question.

If China and Japan compete in military terms, Southeast Asian countries would still be out of the league, and there would remain the question of how they relate as weak powers to stronger regional powers. The problem here is, Asia may be for Asians now, but for which Asians? If you are in a country that is approximately the size of a Chinese province, that question is quite disturbing.

III

What possible problems could emerge in this noncrisis situation based on economics? One problem is that of Chinese nationalism. This is best illustrated by the Spratly Islands and the controversy between China on the one hand and Malaysia, Philippines, Vietnam, Brunei, and Taiwan on the other hand. I do not know on which side Taiwan would fall or if it would fall somewhere in the middle, since China and Taiwan both claim Chinese sovereignty. In any case, China is on one side of the Spratly Island controversy and almost all of contiguous Southeast Asia is on the other.

Why is this controversy so important? From a geographic standpoint, the Spratly Islands are very important to Southeast Asia. If you include the Spratly Islands on a map with China, you also include most of Southeast Asia, because the Spratly Islands are so far south of the rest of China and at the bottom of the South China Sea. This is the problem that Southeast Asians have with the Spratly Islands claim. These islands are at low tide and have a combined area of less than five square kilometers. It is not so much that their claims to these miserable little islands are superior to China's claims, but if China asserts and maintains control over the national sovereignty of the Spratly Islands, China would have power over 80 percent of the South China Sea surface, including the major trade routes that go through the Straits of Malacca up to Northeast Asia.

China's claim worries Southeast Asians in a number of respects. One concern is that in order for China to enforce that claim, it will need a long-range air force and a blue-water navy. Southeast Asia's concern stems from the observation that anything able to defend the Spratlys is able to attack Malaysia or the Philippines, which are the same distance from mainland China.

Perhaps more deeply important for the 1990s are the nationalist implications behind China's claim to the Spratlys. The military's support of China's claim suggests that the military might be in an expansive mood. Even more disturbing is the National

People's Congress's recent reassertion of Chinese sovereignty over the Spratly Islands.

China's actions seem contrary to expectations of what reformers think, and most of the members of the National People's Congress would see themselves as reformers. It was assumed that China would not reassert its claim over the Spratlys because international openness was a major part of China's reform movement in the 1980s, and the Chinese generally touted cosmopolitan over nationalistic aims. I am not sure that this is the case. From new, emerging forces in China, there have been a number of nationalistic moves vis-à-vis Japan and Southeast Asia with the Spratly claims. In any case, why couldn't the forces of China see themselves as part of a young, emergent, and assertive China, a China that more explicitly demands its national interests from countries with which it deals?

With regard to Guangdong province, will its growing international connections and importance make it more understanding of its trade partners, or will it be a reason to assert itself more? Nothing has been decided yet. There will be different forces in the reform movements and the new political dynamics of China in the 1990s, but nationalism is not to be ruled out. Nationalism is not so much a characteristic of Chinese communism as it is a characteristic of where China is in the world and where it sees itself going.

The second possible problem is tied to competition between China and Japan. To a great extent, Sino-Japanese competition has been controlled in the past by the isolation and poverty of China and by the fact that the Japanese economy blossomed beneath an unquestioned American umbrella of military superiority in a bipolar world. Both of these conditions changed massively in the 1980s.

What do these changes imply? For a country like Vietnam, these changes suggest that Hanoi wants the United States back in the region to balance China. Interestingly enough, those in southern Vietnam want the same, but they want the United States in the region to balance Japan. These are two different perspectives on what threatens Vietnam, coming from two very different areas of Vietnam.

In general, however, the potential for competition exists. I am not talking about confrontation between China and Japan, which would be a long way in the future. But at the very least, the implicit competition of military expenditures would place military programs and capacities that are already out of the league of any Southeast Asian country even further away, and would induce catchup military expenditures by Southeast Asian countries that will never catch up. Eventually, it might lead to alliances that would be more exclusive than the current economically based diplomatic relations in the region. Though this is not something that will happen in the next three or five years, it is still a severe, long-term worry for Southeast Asia. These are the kinds of problems that exist in noncrisis situations. It is not a case of the trees falling in the forest and attracting attention, but one of termites in the forest.

What negative developments might occur as a result of such competition? These developments would be characterized by induced militarization, forced choices, and eventually possible threats, but these are a long time off.

The last potentially problematic area between Southeast Asia and China is the relations between China and Vietnam and how those relations may or may not change in the 1990s. This situation has two different aspects. I will begin with continuities. To say that China and Vietnam hate one another is a little too strong, because it implies that the relationship is symmetrical. Vietnam mortally fears China. China despises and resents Vietnam. It is not a very positive relationship. The relationship's asymmetry will continue for a long time to come because it is both an expression of Vietnam's vulnerability to China and China's invulnerability to Vietnam.

China has never worried about the southern barbarians. They have always been considered interesting, but the main threats have been from the north. Vietnam's identity is defined by its independence from China, which is how the country emerged. Regarding continuity, conflicts could develop that might force choices in Southeast Asia but that could also keep Southeast Asia more unsettled and less prosperous as a region than it would be without these conflicts.

Although China and Vietnam normalized their relationships two years ago, their trade is still not normalized. Tensions continue to exist. China, for instance, has been seizing Vietnamese ships on the high seas and impounding their cargos due to alleged smuggling

38

into China through Hong Kong. Vietnam just put 17 major categories of goods on an embargo-impoundment list; that is, these goods are not allowed into Vietnam. If you look at what goods are on the list, you find that they are the primary Chinese export items to North Vietnam. These goods, such as bicycle parts and other items, have destroyed local industry in Vietnam because the Chinese competition is much more efficient. Consequently, there are tremendous tensions and conflicts in the context of an improving relationship between Vietnam and China. Still, it is not at all impossible that at some point in the future those conflicts will instead be in the context of a deteriorating relationship.

The other possible role of Vietnam in the relations between China and Southeast Asia is perhaps more interesting, and it is also more distant. As Vietnam prospers and opens to the rest of the world, it would not surprise me if south Vietnam became more assertive of its interests vis-à-vis the north. Since the national government of Vietnam is controlled by the north and tends to have a northern perspective, separatist tendencies may develop in Vietnam. There is a much greater likelihood of separatist tendencies developing into a major problem in Vietnam than in China.

What this means for China's relationships to Vietnam is a very interesting question. Differences between northern and southern Vietnam may mean different relationships with China. The economy of the north and quite possibly the political relationships of the north will be dominated by Vietnam's relations with China. For southern Vietnam, however, China is not as significant an actor as it is for the rest of the Southeast Asian region, Japan, Taiwan, and other big investors in the south.

The geographical reasons for this are obvious. It is further from Hanoi to Saigon than it is from Chicago, Illinois, to Brownsville, Texas. Vietnam is a very long country—over 1,000 miles from one end to another—and the simple geographical and geopolitical situation of Saigon is very different from the geopolitical situation of Hanoi. If the situation in Vietnam did develop into a conflict, north and south Vietnam's natural pattern of alliances would probably develop very differently. The National government of the north would ally with China and the political power based in the south would ally primarily with other countries in Southeast Asia and with global actors, such as the United States. Given such a situation, there is a clear likelihood of China's unintentional involvement in a potentially serious military confrontation or civil war in Vietnam. That, in turn, could lead to major divisive tensions in the region.

This development, however, is not likely to happen in the near future, because a lot would have to happen before the reemergence of such divisiveness in south Vietnam. At the moment, there are practically no domestic signs of this divisiveness. Having visited north and south Vietnam five times in the last six years, however, I guarantee that there are some resentments in both directions. Hence, the potential for such a situation developing, given the far greater ability of south Vietnam to respond to a world market, is certainly there.

IV

Where does U.S. policy figure in this scenario? My first observation is that the United States is not very significant in this problem. To some extent, the declining role of the United States is inevitable as the Asian economies expand. To some extent it is self-imposed by U.S. foreign policy in the area. The United States isolated itself with its ongoing embargo of Vietnam, and it threatens to isolate itself again from China, given the instabilities or potential instabilities in U.S.-Chinese policy.

As for Southeast Asia, U.S. relations are friendly with all countries except Vietnam. Even our friendly relationships are not close, however, and the countries of Southeast Asia generally do not feel that the United States has the same regional hegemony that it did 20 years ago.

The general policy of the United States toward Vietnam might best be described as "missing." There is no policy toward Vietnam, though the country has been in existence for 17 years, which is longer than the war in Vietnam lasted. Our policy is derivative from the war, and it is a policy of inaction. The United States tends to be slow in responding to Vietnamese efforts, such as cooperation on MIA and POW issues. One thing to do would be to rethink the U.S. position.

The United States might also do what the Australians are doing in Southeast Asia and the world in general, which is to foster relations of mutual economic advantage with other countries in the post-Cold War era. They will do so by supporting their domestic manufacturers and developing markets. By contrast, the United States has developed the habit over the last generation of keying its attention to world affairs by the bipolar political/military struggle of the Cold War. Smaller matters were not worthy of attention in their own right, and our partners were not our equals. But the post-Cold War world is a world of markets, and markets focus on specific economic advantages and opportunities. Big talk will not create markets for America. It needs to develop its industries. The sale of American telecommunications equipment in Vietnam needs to be pushed in the same way that the Australians have been pushing the sale of Australian telecommunications equipment over the past ten years. The failure of the United States to take these actions will mean the deterioration of its position in a post-Cold War environment defined by economics, even as Americans celebrate the victory in the Cold War.

The challenge ahead involves more than determining what will be the new grand vision of the post-Cold war era; it is a question of visual acuity. It is a question of seeing the little things and not reducing every conflict to, and ignoring every opportunity that is smaller than, the mortal military competition between the United States and the Soviet Union.

The third U.S. policy implication is the recognition of the importance of Southeast Asia and the complex roles of Japan and China in Southeast Asia. These factors are unlikely to change. They are realities that Americans will have to deal with in this important area of the world, and unless we understand the complexities of these relationships, we can not deal intelligently with China, Japan, or Southeast Asia.

Until the worst happens and relationships become redefined by military considerations, the U.S. global strategic relationship will continue to be based on the interactions of China, Japan, and Southeast Asia, which are beyond the control of the United States and of which it wants to be a part. A practical implication arising from this observation is that the United States should reduce the pressure for militarization in Asia. Military pressures are unsound for Asia and unsound for the United States, and reduction of those pressures should be a U.S. policy priority. Given our export of military equipment—jet fighters to Taiwan, for example—this change in priorities would require a reversal of several practical U.S. policies.

The change in policy may not make much difference to Charlottesville, where the major exports are apples, wine, and peer-reviewed articles, but in my native town of Fort Worth, any talk about supporting demilitarization in Asia would spark some alarm. The conflict is between near-term interest—in particular, U.S. interest in military exports—and long-term interest, specifically in avoiding a conflictual situation that the United States would not be able to control. One lesson from the war in Vietnam is that U.S. military power is inadequate to enforce our interests in Southeast Asia. If people are going to live in a post-Vietnam-illusion world, then they must understand the complex relationships that exist and become an informed part of them.

QUESTION: Would you say a few words about Cambodia, which is in somewhat of a crisis now, and China's shifting attitude toward Cambodia?

MR. WOMACK: Cambodia is in a miserable situation, and people are suffering, though perhaps not as greatly or acutely as they are in Bosnia. As a regional issue, however, Cambodia has been about 80 percent insulated from the major course of developments in the 1990s. Consequently, Cambodia's problems in the 1990s will tend to be Cambodian problems and to a lesser extent, regional problems.

Beginning around 1990, the Chinese more or less realized that their interest in better relations with Vietnam and better relations with Southeast Asia were more important than their continued support of the Khmer Rouge. As a result, they began a diplomatic retreat from the Khmer Rouge. I do not know how far China has backed away militarily. Chinese foreign policy, especially at the practical level, tends to be very multidimensional. It would not surprise me if some support for the Khmer Rouge still remains.

The Khmer Rouge has become much more dependent on Thailand than it is on China. The Khmer Rouge is selling gems and timber to Thai generals and to other entrepreneurs in Thailand and becoming quite prosperous and very strong in western Cambodia. Chaos, not the Khmer Rouge, is the main threat to the national government, since this government at present lacks the capacity to do anything.

There is a large risk that Cambodia will become partitioned into two parts: a Thai-oriented Khmer Rouge-operated segment of western Cambodia and the rest of Cambodia. At least one more step in that direction will be taken in the next few months when the United Nations decides whether or not to exclude the Khmer Rouge from the elections and again when it see the results of the elections. It is an unfortunate situation in Cambodia, and it is worthwhile for us as Americans to recall that Cambodia is in this situation because we demanded that the Khmer Rouge be included in the country's coalition government.

From the early 1980s, the Vietnamese were happy to have a coalition government excluding the Khmer Rouge. Our insistence, China's insistence, and in a more derivative sense, ASEAN's insistence was that the Khmer Rouge be included. Consequently, in Cambodia today we see the difficulty of including a rabid group of what have become Chinese-supplied mercenaries in a coalition government.

QUESTION: How much central control does the Chinese government continue to exercise over heavy industrial production such as that of steel and cement?

MR. WOMACK: One of the basic changes in China during the 1980s has been a gradual shift away from the centrally controlled economy to, first of all, a more mixed economy, and second, toward a more decontrolled, controlled economy—that is, an economy controlled to a great extent at the provincial rather than the national level. Last year, for example, 50 percent of China's industrial product was in nonstate enterprises for the first time, which means that there is a smaller percentage of production at nationally owned factories in China than there is in India and than there still is in Poland.

There has been a kind of shift, not toward privatization, but away from the centrally controlled Stalinist economic model that has played a large role in the growth of the Chinese economy. It is not quite privatization, because the Chinese are not selling their state assets the way they are in the European post-Communist countries. What has happened is a growth in private and cooperative production rather than a sale and divestiture of state assets.

Second, the provinces are very different. The trade patterns of Guangdong province are both global and within Southeast Asia, which is very different from the trade patterns of an inland province. The individual provinces are allowed to pursue their own interest to a far greater degree than at any other time since 1949.

Economically, China is becoming a much more diverse place, and the political uniformity may today be somewhat misleading. China may have a national governmental structure, rather than a federal structure, but in practical terms, there are limits to what the national government can do now.

QUESTION: With regard to American policy toward Vietnam, one gets the impression from the mass media that a tremendous obstacle to American policy is the perfectionism involved in identifying the remains of those missing in action. Is this the real reason for what you called the "missing" policy of the United States, or is it just a convenient excuse to avoid having a policy on Vietnam?

MR. WOMACK: In 1988 I led a delegation of senior American China specialists to Vietnam, which included Jonathan Pollack of the RAND Corporation. Keep in mind that 1988 was before Vietnam's withdrawal from Cambodia and U.S. policy toward Vietnam was that normalization would take place when Vietnam unilaterally withdrew its forces from Cambodia. Throughout the 1980s, the MIA issue was treated as a humanitarian issue and not as the basis of U.S. policy. Hence, the Vietnamese presence in Cambodia was the one foundation for the embargo and lack of normalized relations. Since the 1978 invasion, the U.S. government has told Vietnam that the United States will normalize when they pull out of Cambodia. Vietnam had options at that time, and they did not have to pull out. Mr. Pollack and I explained and argued for this official position when we talked with our Vietnamese counterparts.

The head of the North American desk at the foreign ministry, however, said, "Things are not so simple. Our presence in Cambodia is the big rock in U.S.-Vietnamese relations, but if the United States moves this big rock, there will be a smaller rock. I do not know what that little rock will be. If that little rock is moved out of the way, there is going to be another rock." Basically, the United States does not want to have relations with Vietnam.

I ran into Jonathan Pollack at a meeting after the Vietnamese withdrew and after the United States added the MIA condition and the condition that Vietnam participate in a comprehensive settlement of the Cambodian question, which Vietnam has also done, in addition to cooperating on the MIA issue. Mr. Pollack and I agreed that the man at the North American desk in Vietnam knew more about the United States than we did.

Given past events, I hesitate to say that the last rock is being removed or that the material issue of those missing in action has been the real problem. There is not much pressure for normalization, because Vietnam just does not seem to be that much of an opportunity. Also, to some extent, it has been a personality issue. In the National Security Council, Kissinger especially is viscerally anti-Vietnamese.

The Vietnamese have opened their military archives to explore the MIA question. They have not demanded a symmetrical opening of U.S. military archives to find out what happened in the last 25 years to the Vietnamese. The United States would refuse. It is a situation where the Vietnamese are doing all they can, not from a desire to see every last MIA family happy, but from a belief that they really need U.S. involvement and from a preoccupation with the question of what more they can do to bring this about. For mainly domestic political reasons and for lack of leadership on this issue, the United States does not want to take a step that might reawaken questions about the Bush administration or the Clinton administration "going soft" on Vietnam. Someone is sure to bring up the issue of remaining MIAs in Vietnam. After all, the French still have MIAs in Vietnam, and there are groups in France too that still say the Vietnamese are holding MIAs and POWs.

QUESTION: What about the boat people that are going to Hong Kong? Why are they leaving Vietnam and what does that do to China?

MR. WOMACK: There are fewer of them leaving now, and that is partly due to the fact that many of them are being returned by Hong Kong. The question of the Vietnamese in China has been a minor question in Chinese-Vietnamese relations over the last few years, but it may become more significant.

The boat people in Hong Kong are now known as the "bus people" because most of them do not take a boat the whole way. What they do is take a bus into China and then a short boat ride into Hong Kong. The bus people are a major headache in British-Vietnamese relations, but the problem is already decreasing and does not involve China.

China's problem with refugees from Vietnam dates from 1978. Vietnam expropriated the property of businessmen in the South (primarily ethnic Chinese) and drove the ethnic Chinese in the North over the border into China. There were 400,000 ethnic Chinese pushed into China. Some of those ethnic Chinese are now returning to Vietnam and demanding their property back.

The Vietnamese negotiators, according to the Chinese foreign experts—not the negotiators themselves—said that the foreign ministry talks leading to normalization did not bring up the question of either reparations or return. Since relations have been normalized, however, several Chinese communiques have questioned what should happen to these former residents of Vietnam that are now in South China. It will be a small issue. It will not break the relationship in itself, but it will be the kind of resentful issue that continues to feed the friction between Vietnam and China.

QUESTION: What effect will Clinton and his possible emphasis on human rights questions have on Sino-American relations?

MR. WOMACK: The question revolves around what type of spin Clinton's foreign policy will be given by the Congress's tendency to emphasize human rights questions. Clinton has said that he does not want to isolate China. If you remember the first debate, Clinton and Perot followed Bush in making this statement. Yet the human rights question and most-favored-nation status in trade relations are both separately—and as linked issues—important for China and for U.S.-China relations.

The American preoccupation with human rights in China places the United States at a disadvantage in their bilateral economic relations with China compared to those countries that do not raise that issue. If the choice is between developing a market for Chinese textiles in Malaysia and developing a market for Chinese textiles in the United States, one consideration will be the threat of possible trade retaliation with the United States.

I would be surprised if the Clinton administration took action with the intent to cause a serious deterioration in relations. Due to careful handling of U.S.-Chinese relations from both the American side and the Chinese side, U.S. officials have managed to avoid a destructive tit-for-tat policy that leads to more deterioration of relations than either country wants. That is, U.S. action might provoke what China would consider a righteous readjustment of policy, only to have the United States find that action a new cause for offense and react further. That pattern of relations and that type of deterioration is by no means impossible.

At a minimum, a Democratic administration will make U.S. policy more adverse to a future Tiananmen-like situation. It will tend to have stronger reactions to a similar event than the Bush administration had to Tiananmen. While the potential for crisis in China will not affect relations with Southeast Asia that much, it will affect relations with the United States. Crisis is by no means inevitable, but Chinese politics faces some hard choices in a post-Deng Xiaoping era.

QUESTION: When Secretary of State Kissinger brought the war with Vietnam to an end in Paris, were there not some severe financial commitments made by President Nixon and Kissinger? Has that been forgotten, or is it still on the table?

MR. WOMACK: It was not forgotten by the Vietnamese until mid-1978. They made reparations a condition on their side for normalization of relations with the United States until about five months before the invasion of Cambodia.

The Carter administration would have been willing to normalize relations with Vietnam earlier had this condition not been attached by the Vietnamese. The Vietnamese were operating from exactly the kind of commitments that you are talking about, but people who worked on this issue in the State Department during the Ford administration were of the opinion that regardless of the commitments, it was politically impossible. Nixon would never have been able to convince the U.S. Congress to agree to fulfill the financial obligations that were agreed to in Paris, especially given the fact that the U.S. official claims that the Paris Accords were being massively violated by the North Vietnamese began in January 1973–weeks after the accords were signed.

The Paris Accords were being violated on both sides, and if one analyzes the Paris Accords, they were made to be violated. The leopard-skin settlement of 1973 has as its only rational explanation getting the United States out of Vietnam. There is no way that the Paris Accords could have been viewed as the blueprint for a peaceful relationship between the forces acknowledged to exist in South Vietnam. What the Paris Accords did do was close the books a bit prematurely on some MIA questions and allow the United States to move out of Vietnam by March 1973. With the U.S. public's shift of attention, the result of resentments about Vietnam and the boat-people issue that began to emerge in 1976, an American administration would not domestically be in a position to execute those agreements.

NARRATOR: We thank Professor Womack for this insightful presentation.

CHAPTER FOUR

China Calls: Paving the Way for Nixon's Historic Journey[*]

RON WALKER AND ANNE COLLINS WALKER

NARRATOR: Anne Collins Walker has been a member of the National Park System Advisory Board and the chairperson of the 1989, 1990, and 1991 HOPE Balls, which are a principal source of fund-raising for Project HOPE. Since 1990, she has belonged to the Women's Board of the American Heart Association, Nation's Capital Affiliate. From 1984 to 1987, she worked as deputy director of public affairs at the U.S. Department of Commerce, and in 1984, she was responsible for delegate, media, and V.I.P. housing arrangements for the Republican National Convention in Dallas. She has also served as special assistant to the chairman and deputy director of congressional relations for the Consumer Product Safety Commission.

Mrs. Walker is the author of *China Calls: Paving the Way for Nixon's Historic Journey.* It tells the story of Ron Walker's first trips to China as President Nixon's director of the White House Advance Office.

Ron Walker is well known in public affairs. He was raised in India, Iraq, Saudi Arabia, and Lebanon while his father was employed by the U.S. government and the Ford Foundation. Mr.

---

[*]*Presented in a Forum at the Miller Center of Public Affairs on 21 July 1993.*

Walker became a captain in the U.S. Army and a graduate of the University of Arizona before becoming president of his own management consulting firm in Dallas.

Currently, he is a senior officer and managing director of Korn/Ferry International's office in Washington, D.C. Mr. Walker has managed numerous CEO and senior executive searches in various industries, including government and quasi-government activities. He has been special assistant to the President of the United States from 1969 to 1972 and director of the National Park Service from 1972 to 1975. While on leave from Korn/Ferry, he served as convention manager for the 1984 Republican National Convention in Dallas. Mr. Walker also serves on the executive committee of the U.S. Olympic Committee, is vice chairman of the Bicentennial of the Constitution and the Executive Committee of the NCAA.

Ron Walker was the first to go to China to pave the way for Mr. Nixon's historic journey to China that resulted in the Shanghai Communique, which Nixon grandiloquently characterized as one of the great historic events. We welcome both Ron Walker and Anne Collins Walker to the Miller Center. We will also have questions and comments from Professors Brantly Womack and Shao-chuan Leng.

MRS. WALKER: In the summer of 1971 when President Nixon appeared on television and told the world that he planned to visit the People's Republic of China, it was a great surprise to everyone, but to Ron and me Nixon's announcement meant that Ron would be going to China. As a child, I was fascinated by all things that were Chinese. I loved Pearl Buck, and I really believed that if we dug long enough, we would find ourselves in China. The thought of beginning a dialogue with people we had not talked to in almost 30 years was rather amazing.

President Nixon wanted to extend a hand of friendship to the Chinese. What is often forgotten is that Nixon began the dialogue with China long before he became president. After losing the governor's race in California, he quietly began to make plans to visit China. When he went around the world in 1969, he stopped in Pakistan and asked to see Pakistan's president, Yahya Khan, privately; no staff were allowed. The U.S. State Department and embassy people could not believe that he had made such an outrageous request. They said that they would not allow it and that their experts would have to be present when the leaders met. Nonetheless, Nixon opened the so-called Yahya Channel during that trip. Thus, a supposedly sick Kissinger on a trip in 1971 had in reality gone to China to set the tone for what had already become a possibility.

The Chinese insisted on dealing with one American for all aspects of the President's trip. That person was Ron Walker, who was a staff assistant to President Nixon and the chief advance man. Ron was in charge of the White House Advance Office and handled all White House travel, domestic and international.

When Ron went to China, he took a team of 100 Americans—television people, technicians, aircraft crews, secret service—all of the different elements necessary to prepare for an international trip for the President of the United States. Ron had to speak for all of them. They knew that they were making history and that the people with whom they would be interacting would not understand our ways, nor would we understand their ways.

The team talked twice a day via a suitcase satellite to Washington. They recorded these conversations, obviously to document everything that was taking place, but also for their historic significance. A complete set of those telephone conversations provides the basis for the book, which is why the book is titled *China Calls*. Since 1972, those conversations have intrigued me.

It took me a year to transcribe 48 reel-to-reel tapes. The sound quality was very atmospheric. The tapes were very difficult to understand and were probably the great-great-great grandfather to what CNN had during Desert Storm, when images were transmitted by satellite and almost immediately received on CNN. When Ron and his team went to China, they had to use equipment that was much less advanced, equipment probably made with first-generation technology. Ron and his team also knew that the Chinese were listening, and because they did not want to appear offensive to them in any way, they were careful about what they said. If the Chinese did not understand some things, Ron and the

51

team were careful to try not to appear critical of that lack of understanding of what the team was asking. In writing this book, I found it fun to put the personalities into the story and to show what was really taking place behind the scenes, apart from the telephone conversations.

Obviously, Ron is the expert in this area; he lived it. I just documented it. Still, the book contains a little piece of history whose details would have been lost otherwise, because the copies of the tapes that are in the National Archives are all edited. Archivists thought that national security was being discussed if the secret service talked, for example. Because I transcribed the unedited conversations, the book documents what really took place.

MR. WALKER: Of the three trips that were made, the next-to-last trip, which has been referred to as the Al Haig trip, was the trip in which we took television technicians along. They were from all three television networks, but not CNN, as it was not yet in existence. There were no satellites or televisions in China. Because everything that we took in would have to be sold to the Chinese, we had many concerns about the Haig trip—concerns about the technicians being with us, how we were going to transmit back to the United States, and under what conditions we would be able to transmit.

Because the Chinese wanted examples and the instructions manuals for everything that was to be set up, we brought huge documents and notebooks that explained what we might do and left these books with the Chinese. There were three possible ways that we could have approached the problem of how to transmit back to the United States. One possibility was to bring in two 747s configurated as a television studio. We would dock them at the Peking airport and travel back and forth between downtown and the airport, which is a 45-minute run one way. The second possibility was to move into an existing facility in downtown Peking and set up our own transmission center there. The third possibility was to build a transmission center, which would include troughs for the cable, interview rooms, sound rooms, and overhead lighting—everything that would be needed for television, especially color television.

Because we had no official dialogue with China and no diplomatic relations, communication was complicated: China would send a message to the Chinese ambassador to France, who was in Paris. From Paris, the signal would then be transmitted to Canadian Prime Minister Pierre Trudeau, who in turn would transmit to us at the CIA. This is the method we used to transmit in those early stages.

When my suitcase satellite went up, the signal would travel from Peking to INTELSAT (International Telecommunications Satellite Consortium), which is the satellite that controls the 160-odd nations around the world, though at that time it was only 53 nations. From INTELSAT, the signal went to Riverside, California. From Riverside, it went to Williamsburg, Virginia, from there to the Department of Defense, and then to the Situation Room in the White House. As a result, there was a 15- to 20-second lag time in addition to the 13-hour time change.

When I arrived in China to begin my 21 days with these 103 men, my counterpart, Ambassador Han Hsu, who was at that time the director of protocol and assistant to Zhou Enlai and later became ambassador to the United States, met me at the airport with a big smile. He said, "Mr. Walker, we have something to show you." After that, we got into our huge motorcade—they were still trying to figure out how to move our equipment, because they were just not prepared for so much of it and apologized for weeks for being unprepared—and drove for approximately three minutes to a brand-new facility. In the two weeks we had been gone, they had literally built the transmission center, complete with cable troughs, lighting, sound rooms—everything was done. After seeing that facility, I have no quarrel at all with the fact that they built the Great Hall of the People in ten months.

MRS. WALKER: The Chinese asked for the owner's manual to every piece of equipment that the Americans brought and then translated each manual into Chinese. Among the many items that Ron and his team introduced to the Chinese, including the copy machine, the most important items were the television equipment—cameras and platforms, for example. The Chinese had a counterpart for every American on the team, and that Chinese counterpart would insist on doing everything his American counterpart did. If one of the Americans put together a television camera, his Chinese counterpart would insist on disconnecting the wire that had just been connected or unscrewing the screw that had just been tightened so that they would be able to say they had put all of that equipment together and that they had built all of the equipment, which indeed they did because it was done twice. Try to imagine the patience that would be required to watch someone undo everything that had just been done. The stress of the job was made worse by the fact that the team had no outlet for any kind of entertainment the whole time it was there. It was freezing-cold, February Peking weather. There were no movies and no television. They could not even go for a walk because there was always someone there stopping them to check what was going on. The Chinese did not know what we were all about, and they just wanted to make sure that they knew what everyone on the team was doing. It became a difficult mental exercise, given the lack of entertainment and social outlets. Also, banquets were long. The Chinese tested the group with all kinds of scary food to see if the Americans would eat it.

MR. WALKER: The Chinese were concerned for our safety when we walked outside or when we went to the Forbidden City, the Temple of Heavenly Peace, or the Great Wall because there were so few Caucasians in China then. As a result, we were never able to leave the hotel without being escorted. At that time there were 800 million people in China, and at times, I believed they were all in Peking. Every time we stepped out of the hotel dressed in our western attire, a large number of Chinese would appear. At that time they only wore one of two outfits, either the blue Mao jackets with the high collar, or the green Mao jackets. Each outfit would prominently display a Mao button on the hat and jacket. They did not necessarily know that we were Americans, and we saw very few other Caucasians in China. We did have minorities in our group. The blacks were just as much an attraction as the Caucasians were. In short, I think their concern for our safety was legitimate.

What we did not know until years later was that the Cultural Revolution was taking place while we were there and that the last emperor had been impounded in the horticultural museum. The Chinese were purging the country's party, government, and army of all opponents to Chairman Mao and purging society of old ideas, culture, customs, and habits. Intellectuals were also purged. It was an interesting time. It was the only time that I had ever set up a presidential event or presidential advance without knowing the outcome. For me, a presidential advance would begin with a phone call from Bob Haldeman or Dwight Chapin about a presidential trip. Whether the trip was domestic or international, a set of criteria would have been determined so that objectives which need to be accomplished are clear.

Once Air Force One lands, all of the arrangements must already have been made. Two planes carrying the press arrive before the president's plane, and on an international trip, outside of China and the Soviet Union, to have 300 or 400 members of the press corps was not uncommon. Many of them are not writers, syndicated columnists, or commentators; they are the technicians that actually make things work. These technicians are responsible for the lighting, the sound, and everything else that takes place behind the scenes.

The office that manages all of the press activities is the White House Travel Office, which was targeted by President Clinton recently. My office coordinated the Secret Service, the White House Communications Agency, Air Force One, the helicopters, the blood plasma—everything that would be needed should a presidential assassination attempt occur.

We did not have the embassy in China at that time, nor did we have the American Chamber of Commerce, or the CIA. One misperception, I think, that the Chinese had all along was that many of us were CIA agents, which simply was not the case.

There was one instance when we found the Chinese to be particularly difficult to work with. They wanted a protocol list in order of precedence of the 391 people who were coming to China. This type of classification, however, is not our way of doing business. How would I rank James Michener, Walter Cronkite and Barbara Walters, and others? We just were not able to do that. We could provide lists of the people in the official party and those in the unofficial party (those from the private sector), but we were unable to rank the people who were not in the government.

I did not have the means to draw up such a list. We had no secretaries. I brought our own typewriters and two military stenos (every member of our party was a male, which was by our own choice at the time) but within ten days, both of them had pneumonia. At one point, we probably had 16 of the 100 people in the Chinese hospital because we were not prepared for that kind of cold. Most of the technicians, having covered football games and similar events, were macho guys, but there was a big difference between Buffalo, New York, and Peking, China. The wind coming off the Gobi Desert could freeze a person.

NARRATOR: So much was made of the secrecy of the Kissinger mission—the use of Pakistan and back-channel operations. Given the fact that you had 100 people, a great deal of equipment and machinery, and were recognizable leaving the hotel, how did you maintain the secrecy?

MR. WALKER: Kissinger did a great job discussing this aspect of the trip in his book. He also takes a great deal of credit for many things that President Nixon did. When Nixon resigned from the presidency and went into exile in San Clemente, California, no one really cared for Nixon, and while there, he almost died. Kissinger took advantage of Nixon's absence and took credit for many things for which President Nixon truly should have been given credit, and I think history will turn that around.

At another time in his career when he was a congressman, Nixon was known as the great Communist hunter. Many liberal Democrats have said that the 1971-72 rapprochement with the People's Republic of China could only have been accomplished by someone like Richard Nixon. Nixon was convinced, he later told me, that if the liberals had known that he intended to attempt the rapprochement with China, they would have done everything in their power to undermine his efforts. That was the rationale behind the secrecy and the rationale behind sending Kissinger to China privately.

Ron Walker and Anne Collins Walker

Kissinger did not see Mao on that trip, but he did see Zhou Enlai. Kissinger wanted to get China's concurrence. During the week we were there, Zhou Enlai said we should be friends. Only one American, Edgar Snow, had been back and forth between China and the United States during the 25 years of isolation. Nixon recognized that there are too many Chinese for us to allow the isolation to continue, and history has proven them right.

From my standpoint, once the trip was announced, it became a matter of how we were going to successfully set up and prepare for the President's trip. Leaving the Oval Office after meeting with President Nixon, Kissinger, and Al Haig, I felt a big lump in my throat. I was only 34 years old, and I realized that the burden was on my shoulders not to botch the President's trip. I can remember thinking that I would be taking people to China and would be responsible for them, but I did not know them. I knew their names but I certainly did not know who they were.

Although many on my team did not like taking orders from a government employee, they soon realized that I was there for only one reason: to make the President's trip a success. If it was a success from the President's standpoint, it would be a success from the network's standpoint. They realized that we were all going to benefit from a successful presidential visit to China, not only as individuals who were on the ground making these preparations but the world as a whole.

Anne's book is wonderful. The story of Nixon's arrival in China has been documented so much, but what she writes about is the story before President Nixon's arrival. She ends the book with snippets from individuals who were covering the event for both television and the print media and with President Nixon's descriptions of the event as "the week that changed the world."

MRS. WALKER: When I told my boss, Malcolm Baldrige, at the Department of Commerce that I was leaving my job to write this book, he was fascinated. He said, "Do you remember what they did to the President when he said that it was a week that changed the world? Everybody laughed! They thought that was a gross exaggeration." Mac Baldrige told me to look at the trade figures, and then he began to cite the numbers of Chinese students who were studying in this country. He said, "I'm proud of the Baldrige years and what we have done with regard to trade with the PRC, and this would not have happened if President Nixon hadn't had the leadership to go to China and meet with the Chinese."

When giant California redwood trees were given as official gifts to China, they were planted all over the country. In later years, they took seedlings from them, and now, they are growing in every province in China. When President Nixon went to China in 1972, not only trees were planted; the seeds of democracy were planted as well. I am convinced of that in light of the events that have transpired.

QUESTION: Having been through one of these presidential missions, I can just barely imagine the problems you encountered. Did many of your party speak Chinese? How did your team work with the Chinese given the language barrier?

MR. WALKER: No, we did not speak Chinese. *Ni hao* (hello) and *xie xie* (thank you) is about the extent of my Chinese. Each of us, however, had a Chinese counterpart who spoke English. In all fairness and with no humor intended, our counterparts spoke to us in 1930s- or 1940s-style English. To give an example, when President Nixon arrived, it was the first time that a full Chinese military contingent, including the honor guard, had been at the Peking airport to welcome a foreign dignitary in ten years. Though we did not know that at the time, we now know that the military contingent was as close as the Chinese could come to letting us know the significance that they placed on Nixon's trip. Upon Nixon's arrival, the military band played "Home on the Range" and "She'll Be Coming Round the Mountain." Some music teacher must have left this music there in 1947, and that is all the Chinese could find to play.

MR. LENG: What was your impression of your counterpart, Han Hsu, in China?

MR. WALKER: Han Hsu is a very slight individual that takes air baths and does 100 push-ups in the morning. He is a remarkable individual, and again, he spoke 1930s-style English. He had gray hair and a crew cut, so he and Haldeman got along very well. Han Hsu is a very direct and serious individual. He would address me as Mr. Ronwalker. It was never two words.

In 1978 Anne and I returned to China as the guests of the Chinese and Ambassador Han Hsu. During that first visit, however, Han Hsu was the director of protocol and the executive assistant to Zhou Enlai. Therefore, when he spoke, I knew that for the most part, he was speaking for the premier. I never met Mao; the only people who saw Mao at the time were President Nixon and Dr. Kissinger. Mao was not in good health, and he was inside the Forbidden City. I did, however, meet with Zhou Enlai on more than one occasion, and he was a remarkable and impressive individual. I think Ambassador Han Hsu took on part of Zhou Enlai's personality. They had been together for so long that they were very much alike.

If they could build a transmission center in two weeks while we were gone, I was convinced that we could get land lines and telephone cabling so that we could start communicating on our telex—at that time we called them TWXes (teletypewriter exchange service); now they are fax machines. I thought that given the right order, someone would flip a switch and suddenly, I would have sound and messages, but unfortunately, the Chinese were testing us every day. For three or four days, I did not see Han Hsu, which was very frustrating. I would be talking to people in Washington and they would want to know why I could not complete the job. I did not know why I couldn't; I just knew that they were not talking to me.

I would not go to sleep until around 2:00 or 3:00 a.m. because we would not be able to complete our telephone calls sometimes until 10:00 or 10:30 at night. Then, we would sit around and talk about the day. It was the only fraternal time we had together, and that sort of kept morale up. I worried about morale a great deal. Men were out by themselves all day. They were under very difficult circumstances, and they had a Chinese counterpart next to them who talked at them all day in English that was 30 years old and sometimes difficult to understand. The jokes did not go over either, so it was a tough time.

Finally, Han Hsu surfaced and called my room. The Chinese would call your room and make an appointment to see you. After arriving, they would then spend the first five to 15 minutes offering you tangerines, Chinese candy, tea—all the amenities complete with graciousness and inquiries about your well-being, such as "Did you sleep well? Did you see a butterfly today? Did you see a rainbow?" As Americans, of course, we wanted to get right to it. We wanted to ask, "What did you come to see me about?" Fifteen minutes later, however, we would still be talking about everything except the actual matter to be discussed.

Finally Han Hsu said, and I am paraphrasing, "Mr. Walker, I understand that you have some concerns." I said that yes, we did; his people were asking for all kinds of information that I was not capable of delivering without the proper mechanisms.

At this point, I realized why they call them "Red Chinese." Han Hsu's face—his cheeks—turned red. He said, "Mr. Ronwalker, we do not know who you are." As I sat there by myself, surrounded by eight or nine Chinese people, all taking notes on his behalf, I thought to myself, "Oh no, he thinks that I'm a spy." I looked at him and said, "Mr. Han Hsu, I cannot imagine that with all of the information you have at your disposal that you don't know what I am. I am an advance man. I blow up balloons. I raise crowds. I am responsible for the logistics for the President of the United States. If you think that I am any more than that, you are wrong."

Han Hsu then said, "Mr. Ronwalker, if we give you this material and technology for your telephone system, we don't know where that will go." He said it could go to the polar bear, meaning Russia. At that point there was great tension on the Sino-Soviet border. I simply said, "Sir, the message will go by satellite, and yes, it can be tapped. But nothing in the message is classified. All I can do is ask that you give me the means by which to do my business." He said, "Thank you very much, Mr. Ronwalker," and they all left.

Interestingly, it was that same night that there was a fire in the Hotel of the Nationalities. It was never reported, but we could have all been killed. The Hotel of the Nationalities was a tinderbox. It was started by one member of our team, a member of the Hughes satellite crew. I arrived at the room first and found a vodka bottle and a roll of marijuana cigarettes. I picked those up, and stuffed them into whatever clothing I had. By that time, the Chinese were all around us. There was smoke down the hall, and we could not see anything. All I cared about was retrieving that satellite, my only link to the outside world. When I reached the satellite room, two military technicians were already there and packaging it up. I sent one message: "This is Roadrunner. There is a fire in the hotel, repeat, a fire in the hotel. We are evacuating immediately. This is Roadrunner out." That was the end of the conversation.

Chapin tells the story later. He remembers walking down the street in Georgetown on a Saturday afternoon when his pager—one of those buzzers—went off. He made a call on a public phone and was told, "Mr. Chapin, we just got a call from Roadrunner. The hotel is on fire and he is down."

During the fire, we realized for the first time that Han Hsu and the vice minister of foreign affairs, Su Long, were living on our floor in the hotel with us. Their presence in the hotel reflected the importance placed on the mission and their desire to make certain that nothing went wrong. Their presence in the hotel, however, also meant that we could have killed them with the fire.

MRS. WALKER: What made the situation worse than it might have been was that the Chinese had padlocked all of the fire exits with chairs and had used the stairwells to store excess furniture—big overstuffed sofas and chairs. It could have been horrendous. The story of the fire is told for the first time in *China Calls*.

MR. WALKER: As a result of the fire, the whole night was lost, but we were supposed to have gone to the Great Wall the next day. Mr. Han Hsu informed me that we would leave an hour later than our appointed time due to the extraordinary evening we had experienced. That next day was a sunny and pretty day, which was unusual for February. When we arrived at the Great Wall, we were like children who had just been let out of kindergarten—Americans running up and down the Great Wall, having a great time, taking pictures of one another. Then, we had this wonderful picnic at the Ming Tombs.

When we returned to the hotel, as often was the case, they said, "Mr. Ron Walker, Mr. Han Hsu would like to have a meeting." I went to see him, and within one hour of our return, the day after the hotel fire, after a great day at the Great Wall, and after thinking that I was a spy, they suddenly decided to give me all of the materials I had asked for. Though it took three or four days to install the equipment and have it running, Han Hsu had talked with Zhou Enlai, and it was agreed that everything was to be made available. There were still some problems, but at least we were able to begin moving the process forward.

We all agreed not to publicize the fire, though we did have one member of the press corps who really wanted to report the story of the fire to one of the networks. The other members of his team, however, convinced him not to report it. Publicizing the fire could have been embarrassing to the Chinese, even though we were the ones that started the fire. What we least wanted to do was cause the Chinese any loss of face or embarrassment because they place much greater importance on that than we do. Fortunately, we were able to keep the story quiet. It never did surface, and it has been 20-odd years now.

MR. WOMACK: I certainly agree with President Nixon that this was a week that changed the world. Besides the diplomatic significance, however, the visit is amazing also because it turned out so well. You deserve much credit for that accomplishment. Not only were there the normal and abnormal difficulties of lacking staff and an unfamiliar place, but there was the additional concern for Chinese sensitivities. At the time, the Chinese were extremely concerned about the implications of having Nixon visit China at a time when their basic diplomatic pattern was one of encouraging revolution and supporting Vietnam. They were also concerned about maintaining their sense of dignity and not being overrun by an American presidential visit. I recall that they insisted that Chinese cars be used for the motorcade, not American cars. I would imagine that you must have experienced Chinese sensitivities in this regard on a daily basis. Do you have any examples?

MR. WALKER: Since Roosevelt's presidency, the Secret Service has moved the president's car to wherever the president went. Once Kennedy was assassinated, however, many dramatic changes took place within the Secret Service. Every place the President of the United States went, both domestic and international, there would be a car-plane that preceded the president. This was a huge aircraft that carried the President's car. In certain cases, there might be more than one car-plane because when the president is traveling to more than one country, the car-planes would leapfrog ahead.

It is a bulletproof car, weighing 10,000 pounds, made by Continental. All four tires could be blown out with a bazooka and it would still travel at 60 miles an hour. It is an extraordinary machine. Also, in some cases—in both China and the Soviet Union, for example—it was the only secure place for the president to have a telephone conversation or a private conversation, because every place in China and the Soviet Union was bugged. Privacy is not assured even when walking through the garden, because they supposedly have microphones in the trees. Only the car offered a secure place.

We did take the car to China, but it was used at the guest house so that President Nixon would be able to talk privately. With the exception of the few personal trips that we made—I think we made six personal trips in that car—we traveled in Chinese cars at all other times. President Nixon also flew on a Chinese airplane during that trip, which was the first time that the President of the United States had ever flown in a foreign airplane. Air Force One flew tandem to it, and we put a suitcase satellite in the Chinese airplane so that communication could take place between the two planes. Because the president is the only one that can order a nuclear attack, the black briefcase must be accessible to him; other countries have more than one person. The President of the United States, being the only person with that authority, needs to be in constant communication with Comsat (communications satellite) and other military installations.

In making the decision to have President Nixon fly on a Chinese airplane, we knew we were changing future history. We knew the Russians were going to want whatever China had and that they would want more of it. In fact, that is what happened. On the President's trip to the Soviet Union, he flew on an Ilyushin 62 from Moscow to Kiev and from Moscow to Leningrad and back on

Russian airplanes. We did, however, use our own car in the Soviet Union.

Regardless of whether the car is foreign or not, the head of the Presidential Protection Detail of the Secret Service always rides in the front seat. This requirement was a point of principle with the Chinese, and we fought with them on that detail until the day the President arrived in Shanghai. We flew to Peking from Shanghai by air because there was no ground transportation in Shanghai, and somewhere between Shanghai and Peking the Chinese finally decided that Bob Taylor could ride in the front seat of the car. They wanted to let us know as a point of principle, however, that they had conceded reluctantly. "The next time you ask for something, Mr. Walker," they said, "you must remember that we gave in on this; we may not give in the next time." They are very nice and they smile, but they are tough about their positions.

QUESTION: With regard to Chinese negotiating style, were there any other incidences similar to the one that you just mentioned where the Chinese would concede on a certain point only to remind you of it later when discussing a different and separate point?

MR. WALKER: There is another instance of such a case. I do not like to talk about it because it involves a hairdresser, a current point of controversy with regard to the Clintons. We had an argument with the Chinese over a hairdresser for Mrs. Nixon. (Mrs. Nixon was a wonderful lady and one of the greatest first ladies that this country has ever had. When she passed away recently, I made the funeral arrangements on behalf of the President.) The problem we had with the Chinese centered on the number of people that we planned to bring to China. Originally, we intended to bring 310 or 320 people, but the number increased to 391. Keep in mind that the greatest number of people ever brought to China by any head of state in 25 years was 14. To them, it must have seemed as though we were bringing a city.

Part of the problem, too, was that we kept changing the numbers. We would prepare scenarios for each movement and give it to the Chinese, and the next day, it would be returned to us translated into Chinese. All of the changes were not appreciated by the Chinese, and every time we changed the numbers, they would let us know that it was not proper for us to change the number on which we had already agreed in principle.

The last straw came when I asked the Chinese to add one more person to the manifest. I had received a late request to include a hairdresser for Mrs. Nixon—in those days we called her the personal assistant to the first lady—because we were uncertain as to whether there would be any hairdressers available in China. The request came during the final hours of negotiation over the details of the trip; everything was locked in. Upon receiving the additional request, the Chinese made certain that I knew they had had enough. I'm convinced that the Chinese had a good chuckle after meeting with me because they knew that they had gotten me.

One other point is that during these midnight raids on my room when I would be summoned by the Chinese, I would have to get dressed and go to another sitting area. There would be a half dozen Chinese there and they would have a few questions—some of them trivial, some important, and some for which I did not have answers. Not until much later did we realize that Zhou Enlai slept during the day and worked during the evening; thus, my interrupted evenings could be attributed to Zhou's personal interest in the trip. The questions originated with him and ended up in my bedroom. The next thing I knew, I was down the hall answering the questions, and they were going back to the prime minister with the answers. Thus, I felt much better that it was not necessarily harassment; it was legitimate in many instances.

NARRATOR: Recently, Larry Eagleburger said that the most important question of the future may be whether or not China can make the transition from an open and free economy, or the beginnings of it, to a politically free society. When he and Brent Scowcroft went to China on a secret mission, which was not such a secret, they came to believe that China would move in that direction. He said that as time goes by and as he sees changes taking place, he thinks that sometime in the future, although perhaps not in his lifetime, China will move politically in the direction that it has economically. In terms of China's development, did you have any idea of what would be the next step after Nixon's visit when you were there in 1972?

MR. WALKER: I do not think that I had an idea when we left in 1972. Not until 1978, when Anne and I returned to China did I feel that the seed, what Anne refers to as democracy coming, had been planted. At that point, I had been the director of the National Park Service. We went to Hangzhou, which is very similar to northern California, where the giant redwoods grow. I remember talking with the forester who was in charge of the redwoods in Hangzhou about Zhou Enlai's visits to the area during recent years and about how the strength of the Sino-American relationship had its basis in the roots of the redwood trees planted there. Now that they are in every province, the seed of friendship between the United States and the People's Republic of China will continue to grow.

Until the Tiananmen Square incident, which was a huge setback, there was no doubt in my mind that we would see a more public side of Chinese democracy before the year 2000. The Tiananmen Square incident, however, set back the process considerably. I'm not certain that I will see the transition in my lifetime either.

MRS. WALKER: I remember Ron asking how the Chinese would be able to keep such a strong communist regimentation when the tourists began to arrive. Ron did not think that the Chinese would be willing to continue living such Spartan existences once they saw the affluence of those who visited their country.

I remember visiting China's schools and seeing nursery school children with clenched fists and strong determination singing in praise of Chairman Mao. They would not meet my eye or smile at me, and I could not help but compare them to school children in America who giggle and hit each other when performing a play. The children in China never wavered at all. The indoctrination was so incredible. Tiananmen Square obviously erupted because they could no longer keep everything to themselves.

When the Tiananmen crackdown occurred, we were very concerned about Han Hsu, who was the Chinese ambassador to the United States during that time. He had been advising his government when he was suddenly recalled to China. We were very worried because during his stay in the United States, Han Hsu had become a little Americanized; we did not know what he might have been saying to his government at the time of the crackdown. Fortunately, he has since corresponded with us, and we are grateful that he is alive and well.

MR. WALKER: I have noticed some changes in the Chinese since 1971 and 1972. On the Haig trip, for example, General Haig's secretary had thrown a pair of panty hose in the trash. As we were boarding the buses to leave for the airport, a floor attendant came running out with a little plastic bag and handed the panty hose to General Haig's secretary, who was embarrassed to tears. What is significant about that episode is that it demonstrated the honesty of the Chinese. If someone left something, they returned it; that was their way. When we went back to China in 1978, however, that standard had changed. In 1972 the Chinese would have never taken anything, but in 1978 a driver asked to see my roll of film and never returned it to me. I did not ask for it back because I was curious to see what he would do. We never saw the driver again. In 1978 China had already begun to change, and it has changed dramatically ever since then, especially in Shanghai and along the southern coastal areas near Guangzhou.

QUESTION: I understand that someone thoughtlessly set fire to a couple of trucks with Chinese soldiers in them. How much was the trouble in Tiananmen Square the result of overzealous demonstrations for democracy?

MR. WALKER: I'm not certain about the exact circumstances around what happened internally in China. I have heard similar stories about the military being attacked and how students were out-of-line and rebellious in many cases. Personally, I do not think that their rebelliousness was responsible for the massive display of power that was brought down on those students.

QUESTION: In 1972, was there any discussion about a seat in the United Nations for the People's Republic of China?

MR. WALKER: President Nixon and Zhou Enlai discussed the People's Republic of China's role in the United Nations. Though China became a member of the United Nations and the Security Council by October 1971, they calculated that it would take a minimum of five years—beginning with the Shanghai Communiqué in 1972—for the normalization of Sino-American relations to be complete. Not until the Carter years, after a whole series of events had taken place, congressional resistance had been overcome, and Ping-Pong diplomacy had run its course did the normalization of Sino-American relations finally take place.

QUESTION: In Zbigniew Brzezinski's latest book, he writes that China is now possibly the second largest economy in the world after the United States. I do not know if Hong Kong is included in that calculation. Do you have any information about their economic growth?

MR. WALKER: I have not read his book, but I have read the synopsis, and I think he does include the Hong Kong figures. More important, given the industrial zone between Shanghai and Guangzhou and investment from Taiwan and the United States, from an industrial standpoint China is, if not the second largest economy, certainly among the top five economies, and it is still growing.

MR. WOMACK: On this specific point, the World Bank figures released yesterday ranked China third behind the EEC and the United States, which were pretty much tied. Japan followed China, and then far behind Japan was the Soviet Union. Therefore, if the EEC countries are considered one unit, then China's economy is the third largest, but if they are considered individually, then the ranking order would be as follows: the United States, China, Japan, and Germany.

MR. LENG: The Chinese leaders are trying very hard to deny their high ranking, however, because they want to keep their under-developed status so they can get loans from the international banks. Also, the current problems of inflation and the overheated economy are causing a great deal of concern. The good thing, however, is that Zhu Rongji, who is the vice premier, is now in charge. In contrast to the sick premier, Li Peng, Zhu Rongji is a reformer. China's economic problems may be a blessing in disguise, because if Zhu Rongji can successfully manage China's economy, he will be promoted and Li Peng will be defeated.

MR. WOMACK: The reason for the paradox of China's sudden leap from a poor country to rich country in the statistics is that the basis for calculating economic productivity has changed. Instead of calculating the size of China's economy by the official exchange rate, by translating renminbi into dollars, it is now calculated by measuring the purchasing power of the renminbi within the Chinese economy. Within China, the renminbi purchases a tremendous amount of goods. For example, a teapot can be bought for a dollar in China. In a certain respect, therefore, the Chinese economy appears to be very prosperous. China, however, still has a relatively weak currency, and in many respects China is a poor country, not only per capita, but as a national economy. Nonetheless, the new method of calculating the size of the economy does take into account the monetary difference.

MR. LENG: Structural change in the financial system will also be very necessary.

NARRATOR: Before the Forum, I asked Ron Walker how he would like to be introduced. He said to tell the audience that he has been married to Anne Collins Walker for 35 years and that they have three lovely daughters, and while he did not make this next statement, he did imply that they would also live happily ever after. After watching this remarkable interplay between husband and wife, it is easy to understand why he asked for the introduction that he did. We are grateful to both of you for coming.

CHAPTER FIVE

China in the 1990s: Three Perspectives*

INIS L. CLAUDE, JOHN ARMITAGE, AND SHAO-CHUAN LENG

NARRATOR: We welcome you to an inquiry on China. John Armitage and Inis Claude have just recently returned from trips to the People's Republic of China, and Shao-chuan Leng virtually commutes back and forth between Charlottesville and China. Our three colleagues are here to share their impressions of China in the 1990s.

Professor Leng came early to the Miller Center when we thought it would be appropriate to add at least one comparative dimension to our program. In addition to being the president of almost every one of the China and Asia professional societies, he has been the chairman of the Asian Studies Program at the University of Virginia. He is largely responsible for the interest in China and the growth of competence in China studies at the University of Virginia. He has been the major figure in the promotion of China studies at this university.

Professor Claude was for many years the professor of international relations, institutions, law, and politics at the University of Virginia. He is a world-renowned leader in the study

---

Presented in a Forum at the Miller Center of Public Affairs on 2 July 1993.

of international relations. Rarely has the retirement of two people been as great a loss as it was when Professors Claude and Leng retired. Fortunately, they have continued to be active and have participated in a great many programs.

As for Jack Armitage, he was deputy assistant secretary of state for European affairs. He has served in the former Soviet Union, Czechoslovakia, and the Middle East. He has had wide experience and has served as diplomat-in-residence for several years at the university and as a professor after that time. He, too, has recently returned from China.

MR. LENG: My task today is to chair the meeting and to comment on the observations of my two colleagues. Professor Claude will begin the session and Jack Armitage will follow.

MR. CLAUDE: As indicated, Jack Armitage and I are the inexpert commentators on China today. We are rank amateurs with only a touristic knowledge of China. We went to China with great interest in what we might discover there, and we came back very excited about what we did observe. Our recent exposure to China has only stimulated our interest, and as a result of that exposure, we bring with us many impressions, observations, puzzlements, and questions.

During my time in China, I was impressed by China's passionate efforts to attract the Olympic Games to Beijing in the year 2000. When we arrived at the Beijing airport, there were banners, placards, lights, and billboards—all of them proclaiming, "A more open China eagerly awaits 2000 Olympics." These signs were everywhere in the city, and it is evident that China is all agog about the prospect of being host to the Olympic Games in the year 2000.

Shanghai gave us a foretaste of what the Olympics in Beijing might look like. When we began our tour in Shanghai, the city was preparing to play host to the East Asia games, a kind of regional Olympics. Though the games did not begin until one or two days after we left Shanghai, while we were there the city was already involved in all of the preparations—the extra lights, banners, and flags.

"A more open China awaits the 2000 Olympics." The Chinese are obviously interested in the prestige that goes with playing host.

They are interested in the large influx of people who will visit China as a result of the Olympics and in what they hope will be the economic advantage of playing host to the Olympic Games. One hopes that the preparations which are already in progress will provide long-term value to the people of China. For instance, the prospect of hosting the Olympic Games has prompted the construction of a major expressway between the airport and the city of Beijing. On this magnificent new highway leading into the city, outsiders will catch their first glimpses of China.

There is an impressive openness about China now. In the previously mentioned Olympic slogan, there is an implicit promise to become more open, and that undoubtedly is an attempt to attract the Olympic Games. It is a way of saying, "If you would just give us the Olympic Games, we will promise to be a more open society." The Chinese have a genuine urge to be a society more accessible to the rest of the world. The openness evident to the tourist is already substantial. There are tourists everywhere in China, and they come from all over the world—Asia, Europe, America. Every hotel room that we encountered had a CNN television hookup, so we were connected to the world. I do not know how much exposure to the foreign press and television the ordinary people of China get, but certainly the tourists—and I would expect the intellectuals and elite groups in Chinese society as well—have a good deal of access to outside communications by way of television and other instruments of modern communication. In short, the tourist at least gets the impression that China is eager to join the world. Furthermore, I would expect this increasing openness and increasing exposure to the outside world and its ideas, culture, and way of life—exposure that is exhibited also in the fast-food chains coming into China—would have a significant long-term, and perhaps even short-term, impact on the political system.

Frankly, given today's world and its virtually unstoppable wave of communication, I do not see a real possibility of anything remotely approaching what we used to call totalitarianism—the total regimentation of society, the total control of central authority over what is said, done, and imagined within a society. There may be more of that in China today than meets the tourists' eye. As a tourist, I am not an expert in detecting the main aspects of a closed,

73

repressive, quasi-totalitarian system. Nevertheless, I had the impression of an increasingly open society, and that openness inevitably will have some consequences for their political system. For instance, I would judge that the exposure to the outer world will surely impede and undermine any efforts to maintain major political controls on the entire society.

In addition to China's passion for the Olympic Games, my wife and I also noticed that China is engaged in an extraordinary economic boom. I should note that we visited only major cities and merely glimpsed the nearby countryside. Also, for the most part, we only saw the eastern edge of China, particularly to the southeast. Nevertheless, the economic system seems to be adapting, growing, and reforming itself. There is an emergent Chinese capitalist/ communist system in the process of development. Southeast China would indeed seem to be involved in something approaching an economic miracle, as we have come to call it.

When we were in Hong Kong, which was our last stop, we detected a revival of confidence there. I had been led to believe in previous years that Hong Kong was skittish and nervous about the impending political unification with China, and undoubtedly some of that nervousness still remains. Nevertheless, there is an air of renewed confidence in Hong Kong. One almost got the impression that Hong Kong expects to take over China, rather than China taking over Hong Kong. That is an exaggeration, of course, but a "Hong Kongization" of southeast China is well underway. Guangzhou, the area formerly called Canton, is rapidly becoming another Hong Kong. That type of economic development is clearly taking place.

It would appear that the Chinese people have an entre-preneurial bent and talent that perhaps distinguishes China from the Soviet Union. At least the vendors, with regard to the tourists, are not at all shy about pushing the profit motive along.

The question arises in my mind as to whether China is the one communist system that can and does adapt, reform, and modify itself and thus is the only one likely to survive. We have seen the collapse and utter failure of communist systems by and large. China may be the exception to the rule. Is China successfully doing today what Gorbachev wanted to do, hoped to do, tried to do, but could not do in the Soviet Union? At any rate, to the simpleminded tourist, the economic and social systems do not show any signs of breaking down or falling apart. They seem to be in a boom condition.

Obviously, there are political implications and foreign-policy implications of that economic development that we may want to consider. Among other things, there is clearly going to be much stronger resistance to American pressures and threats to take away China's most-favored-nation (MFN) status than one might otherwise have expected.

MR. ARMITAGE: The first general remark that I have about China is that China is a country on the move. The energies of its people are now being freed up, and China will be a major factor in world affairs beginning now. Second, the Chinese are justly proud and quite clearly conscious of their own long history of surviving as a people for over 3,000 years. They have a culture with beliefs, values, and modes of conduct that they treasure, and they will alter them only by their own choosing. Our leaders and policymakers, who are unfortunately as ignorant of China as we are, will need to make strenuous efforts to try to understand and respect this very complex people and nation if the United States is to avoid the kind of serious mistakes in policy that could have far-reaching, adverse effects on its interests in Asia and throughout the world.

I am not going to make an ordered analysis, but I do have a few observations that might have some relevance as to whether China will be inclined to work out its mutual relations with the United States and other nations through serious negotiations and mutual accommodation, or whether this country is headed for some measure of strain and confrontation. My brief observations there would support the contention that there are strong impulses in China seeking to work out relations with the United States through serious negotiations.

Of all the things that my wife and I saw in China, the most fascinating and the most interesting was not the Forbidden City, not the terra-cotta soldiers buried by the emperor, not the Ming Tombs, not even the Great Wall. The most interesting phenomenon we saw was bicycle traffic! Everyone rides a bicycle in China—grandmothers, young women in miniskirts, young bureaucrats dressed up for a conference. We also saw bicycles loaded down with bathtubs and pianos. The most interesting bicycle we saw had a long sofa with a child sitting on each end positioned behind the bicycle seat. Amazingly, we observed only one accident. The people are just as determined to get where they are going as we are in the United States. But the number of bicycles on the street requires that the distance between two bicycles be no more than one foot, so all proceed with deliberate speed and careful attention. The one thing that no one on a bicycle ever does in China is to make a sudden turn. A person gets where he or she is going by making very modest turns.

I observed one incident involving a woman riding a bicycle who noticed a man on her left trying to cut in front of her. Instead of dodging him, however, she made some careful calculations, maneuvered her bicycle slowly to the left, cutting him off, and the man surrendered. Despite the speed at which they are all moving, accidents are few because everyone understands and abides by the rules of the road. They know when they can move ahead and when they have to drop back. It occurred to me that there might be an analogy to be made here between China's bicycle traffic and China's conduct in international relations. The Chinese might be more willing to play the game if they could be fairly certain that everyone is bound by the same rules—rules that they have had a part in devising.

Second, China's Confucian ethic, which dominated the behavior of government and all aspects of life, is not a religion but a comprehensive ethical system extending back over a thousand years. It was hierarchical, but those in authority were expected to fulfill certain obligations if they were to retain their authority. Buddhism, on the other hand, is not indigenous to China, but the Chinese have made it distinctively Chinese—a Buddhism different from that of anywhere else. Remarkably, Buddhism—and Taoism also—do not appear to have any trouble coexisting with Confucianism, despite their contradictions. China's religious tolerance was striking to me, particularly given the history of Western culture: of the Hundred Years War, the Crusades, the Protestant-Catholic wars. In contrast, I am very impressed by the fact that China has *no* history of religious wars with all of their fervor and casualties.

Another interesting characteristic of the Chinese is their willingness to learn from others and their way of giving their newly acquired skills and knowledge distinctively Chinese characteristics. When China came into the United Nations, for example, I watched with great interest China's efforts to learn how it operated. Though China had been excluded from the United Nations, and though the United Nations was the political instrument that had authenticated their isolation from the international community, China did not enter the United Nations contentiously. Instead, the Chinese were avid inquirers, asking everyone how business there was conducted. As a result, they learned quickly.

This Chinese willingness to ask questions and to learn was very different from the way the Russians would have approached the situation. Compared to the Russians, the Chinese are confident in the vitality and legitimacy of their own belief system, and being able to trace that belief system back through the centuries with a certain continuity, they feel no need to prove themselves to others. The Russians, on the other hand, could never admit that they did not know something, so they could not ask others. They would get all of the necessary books, and they might even send out their spies to gather information, but they would not ask. The Chinese would take what others had to teach them and make it their own.

There are some indications, stemming from tensions in two specific areas, that China might become an assertive, nationalistic, and even confrontational player in the international realm. Politically exploited, these tensions could be powerful forces pushing China toward a less cooperative stance. The first area of tension is the growing regional, socio-economic disparities between northern and southern China. Nature seems to have drawn a line across the middle of China, right above Shanghai, creating two different Chinas. Below that line, water is plentiful and everything is lush. Much rice is grown there. North of that line, the terrain is harsh. While the Yellow River does overflow to allow the growth of some crops in the north, rice is still not one of them. Invigorated by reform efforts, southern China will continue to develop much more rapidly and much more vigorously than the northern part of the country. The government will certainly make some effort to pour investments into the north to modify the disparities and to help the north develop. It will try to establish other enterprise zones. One such zone has been set up in the north and touches Korea, Manchuria, and Russia. It is going to be interesting to watch what happens. It is probable that the difference in prosperity, well-being, and the rate of development between the south and the north is going to become more and more marked.

A bid for greater political power is certain to be made as a consequence of the south's increasing economic vitality. This is already apparent in a number of ways, and it is likely to challenge Beijing's claim to be the dominant political center in China. No one gives up power easily or happily, and the potential for conflict between the north and the south is tremendous. It is not hard to see how uneven economic development, which overlies the feeling that many Chinese values are being eroded by this influx of Western influence, has caused some resentment. Hard-pressed political leaders, whether they come from the north or the south, might find it necessary or feasible to appeal to that nationalist sentiment to stay in power.

Second, I see similar differences in development between the country and the city. Development of the countryside began vigorously in the early years of reform, but its progress has now leveled off, if not stagnated. There have also been strikes in the villages. With their newfound freedoms, villagers have come to resent the levies, fees, and other kinds of extortion that the local bosses have imposed on them. The central government has apparently been somewhat reluctant to promote the technology necessary to make the countryside much more efficient. If China is to be more prosperous, however, it will have to invest heavily in the countryside. There will be an increasingly substantial flow of people moving to the cities, and that will only exaggerate the cities' disparity between the rich and the poor.

All of the factors I mentioned could become powerful pressures for an assertive kind of nationalism that might even be prepared to risk confrontation.

MR. LENG: I am in general agreement with my colleagues' comments, but I would like to amplify some points and also to comment about the status of China today. Regarding religious tolerance, the Chinese people are very pragmatic. They want to get the best of everything that comes to their attention. They do not want to put all of their spiritual eggs into one basket, and this will probably be reflected in their approach to so-called communism as well, which is almost a dead issue. No one in China takes communist ideology seriously. Everyone knows that communism is bankrupt.

In the recent convening of the National People's Congress and the parliament in March, the Chinese leadership revised some provisions of the constitution by replacing the phrase "planned economy" with "socialist market economy," which is very important. Today in China, the Chinese talk about a socialist economy or "socialism with Chinese characteristics." How is socialism defined in this context? According to Chinese explanations, everything that promotes development and a higher standard of living is "socialism." Actually, it is capitalism.

Since the Tiananmen massacre, starting in 1990, the Chinese leadership has begun to make changes, particularly evident last year when Deng Xiaoping went to the south to urge the speeding up of economic reform. This is part of the vast capital investment, stock market speculation, and real estate boom in China. Since last year, the Chinese economy has grown at a remarkable rate of 12 to 14 points. Industrial growth is up approximately 21 or 22 percent. The privatization and globalization of the Chinese economy are also more visible. Time does not allow me to give details, but bear in mind that this privatization and globalization is already taking place in China.

The Chinese economic boom has reached such proportions that this year the World Bank, after devising a new calculation of national wealth, listed China as the second largest economy—directly after the United States. The International Monetary Fund was more cautious and listed China as the third largest economy behind the United States and Japan. In short, there is no question about the Chinese economy continuing its current pace. Like Japan, China will someday become one of the economic superpowers.

China's economic growth, however, does not obscure the fact that China still has a big problem. It is precisely because the growth is so fast that China now has the problem of an over-heated economy, which in turn has produced high inflation. This was evident during my visit to China this spring, and it worried me. I saw the fancy shopping centers and supermarkets—one shopping center in Shanghai seemed even more reminiscent of the United States than China. Despite the seeming prosperity, the cost of living this year rose approximately 17 percent, and retail prices rose 21 or 22 percent.

In 1981, when I was a member of the American Bar Association delegation to China, I had the pleasure of talking with the mayor of Shanghai, Jiang Zemin. He is now a current leader in China, and his many offices include head of state and head of the party. In 1981 I was quite impressed not so much by his knowledge of state affairs but by his language capacity. He was a showcase, trying to impress me with his ability to speak English, Russian, Japanese, French, and other languages. Nevertheless, I must say that I found him rather shallow. Jiang Zemin is one reflection of China's problem with leadership. He can get by as long as he follows Deng's line and the advice of other leaders.

During my visit this spring, I also had dinner with the current mayor, Huang Ju. He is a man of sophistication and has aides everywhere in Shanghai who are very impressive. These aides speak with much knowledge about high technology and international economics, among other things, and are a few of China's better leaders, particularly among the regional leaders.

Fortunately, Li Peng, the current premier and also the most unpopular person in China, is quite sick and probably will not be around much longer. There is a joke in Beijing that during Tiananmen some people held up signs in protest against Li Peng. Some of these signs said that Li Peng must resign because he had not done much for the country. Others said that Li Peng was a fool and should step down. All of the protesters were taken into custody by the police, and were tried for their actions. Those who held up the first sign were sentenced to 15 years in prison for insulting a leader; those holding the second sign, however, were sentenced to

30 years. Everyone asked, "How come?" The judge answered, "Because the second group revealed a state secret."

China is also experiencing increasing problems with its peasant population. Peasants initially benefited from Deng Xiaoping's reforms; however, in recent years the attention has turned to the coastal areas and the urban centers. Available funding has been concentrated on new development at the expense of the peasants. As a result, peasant incomes have grown only 0.3 percent annually in recent years. Furthermore, the amount of arable land has declined because some was used for much-needed housing projects and for industrial development. Many peasants, however, had used this land for rural or township industries (which contributed one-third of China's GNP). You can see why there were reports of peasants rioting in certain provinces. Currently there are 70 to 100 million people who are part of the so-called floating population from the rural areas moving from one region to another and from one city to another seeking better jobs. As a result of these factors, the Chinese Communist Party finds itself no longer able to control the populace. Political change is, therefore, bound to happen.

Compounding China's troubles is the accompanying problem of corruption. One-third of the 100 million state employees are also engaged in some kind of business or part-time job, but many of them take advantage of their connections or positions. As a result, economic crimes such as embezzlement and bribery have become serious problems. Statistics show how seriously the government is trying to attack these corruption issues.

In short, the Chinese regime is now confronted with many problems—problems that some people say existed in 1989. The situation has changed since then, however, and conditions are perhaps somewhat improved. Just two days ago the vice president of the World Bank expressed some concern about China's situation, but he also said that the Chinese leaders are aware of the problems and are already taking measures to cope with the overheated economy, inflation, and high interest rates. Should the situation get much worse, the Chinese can also take stronger measures such as curtailing investment and tightening credit to cope with the situation.

I am optimistic about China's ability to cope. At a conference in Washington that I attended last week, we discussed these problems. Most of those in attendance seemed to agree that the problems China now faces are not as serious as those faced in 1989 when the Tiananmen massacre occurred, because the Chinese economy has greatly improved since then. The building of infrastructure is under way; national or domestic saving is at a rate of 30 percent of the GNP; and the influx of foreign capital, particularly from overseas Chinese, continues to increase.

When one compares China with the former Soviet Union, one has to be more charitable with the Russians because they are not used to trading like the Chinese. They were under communism too long. China was under communism for only about 40 years. Also, Russians do not have the advantage of overseas Chinese, whose investment in and devotion to China is very impressive.

These factors—China's developing infrastructure, domestic saving, foreign investment, and rapid increase of foreign imports—will help China overcome her current problems, which are being dealt with by some of the Chinese leaders more capable than the premier. China should be able to maintain its rate of growth at 7 or 8 percent. If that continues into the next century, China will certainly emerge as one of the world's economic superpowers, if it is not one already.

QUESTION: Of all of the comments you made, the most impressive to me is the conflict between the rapidly progressing, modern city and the huge, colossal part of China that is still old China. Inflation only makes the situation worse when its broad impact reaches huge areas that have no way of adjusting. Isn't this a basis for a tremendous social problem?

MR. LENG: Yes it is. In recent months the Chinese have convened many meetings to deal with rural problems. For example, they decided to lower the taxes and to ask the local authorities not to make further demands on the peasants—for example asking for their contributions to economic and social activities—so that their burden might be lessened.

I also understand that they are now also trying to move some investment from the coastal areas into the interior rural areas to help rebuild the confidence of the peasants. The problems are certainly there, but as many economists say, they are manageable and China is trying to address them.

QUESTION: There has been some effort to increase the number of permanent members on the U.N. Security Council by two— namely, Japan and Germany. How is China, as a permanent member, likely to vote on that issue?

MR. CLAUDE: It is hard to guess what China's reaction to that proposal is. Increasing the Security Council membership has other problems, of course. If the aim is to have a directorate of great powers, Japan and Germany would belong there. One of the difficulties, however, is that the rest of the world will immediately chime in with talk of other continents needing representation on the list of permanent members. Increasing the Security Council, therefore, may be opening a Pandora's box, resulting in the inordinate enlargement of the Security Council. I think that would be deplorable—the Security Council needs to be a relatively small body. China would be particularly concerned about Japan's entry, but it is uncertain whether their objection would stem from historical grounds or from rivalry and uncertainty about relationships within Asia.

NARRATOR: Would it be feasible to establish another body with a somewhat different status than that of the Security Council, to be made up of six additional countries and one or two more major nations?

MR. CLAUDE: There has been some possibility of that. The United Nations has considered various ways of juggling the enlargement process to make the Security Council a more realistic reflection of the real importance of the major states of the world. There might be, for instance, a semipermanent membership such as that which the League of Nations Council developed at one stage of its existence. Whether that would satisfy the other nations, however, is hard to say. The basic problem is how to achieve appropriate representation in the Security Council without enlarging it so much that it becomes almost another General Assembly. The United Nations has not solved problem that yet.

QUESTION: Professor Leng suggests that economic development will bring about political change in the future, but isn't it just as possible China will experience political chaos instead of stability in the future? Do you think stable political development requires first the expansion of political interest and then the channeling of that rising demand? If the agent for this kind of channeling is the political party, what is the capacity of the Chinese Communist Party to be that channel? Moreover, if it is unable to meet the challenge, what are China's alternatives in the foreseeable future?

MR. LENG: This question is interesting and difficult to answer. Professor Robert Scalapino of Berkeley has a name for this future channel: authoritarian pluralism. This is sort of a contradiction, but it actually may describe China's political situation well. In March, the Chinese revised their constitution. In one provision, the new wording is "multiparty cooperation and consultation under the leadership of the Chinese Communist Party." This precisely pertains to Scalapino's terminology. It is authoritarian pluralism— pluralism under the guidance of the Chinese Communist Party.

China's political liberalization is gradually taking place, but it will take much longer than China's economic reforms. Nevertheless, the economic reforms will facilitate China's political liberalization; China's reforms have progressed too far, and there is no turning back to the past. China is heading toward what some of the conservative Communist leaders in China fear most—the so-called peaceful revolution of China. The pluralism of Chinese society today is already in evidence. Inevitably, China will need political change.

Whether there will be political chaos, revolt, or peaceful transformation, no one can say with certainty. If the current policy continues and the door to the outside and to the West remains open, China's peaceful transformation will take place. The availability of modern communication tools make it impossible for China to return to the days of Mao Zedong.

QUESTION: Continuing on that point, I would like to ask Mr. Claude what he thinks the impact of China's increasing openness will be on China. Did you see a large influx of Western popular culture or foreign investment when you were there? Do you think it is a positive or negative impact? Did you detect any hostility toward these outside influences?

MR. CLAUDE: I did not detect any hostility; there may be some, of course. Everything I saw indicated pride and happiness about China's openness to the world. All of the hotels at which we stayed were joint venture hotels, involving Western or Hong Kong capital. The largest crowds we saw were the mobs of people overflowing the stock market building in Shanghai.

There seems to be great enthusiasm for the reported benefits of economic development; thus at the moment, it seems that China is encouraging and welcoming Western influences, although they are bound to lead to great change in the political and social systems of China. If one were a rigid dictator, he should be terribly worried about these developments, but on the contrary, in China there appears to be a pragmatic emphasis running through the new political forms. One must not take the view that there are only two kinds of political systems possible in the world: the rigid dictator-ship and the democratic way of life. There are many kinds in between the two, and I would be very hesitant to guess where on the spectrum China's political system will fall in the short term, or even the long term.

QUESTION: My question is also about China's economic growth. We talk about how the open economy will lead to political change and the "Hong Kongization" of southeast China. As Hong Kong has been known to be very money-oriented, is southeast China becoming the same? Or is there a larger sense of public purpose among the people? Also, is there a difference between the message the leadership is sending—in terms of "Here is an open China"—versus the people themselves?

MR. LENG: I must confess my bias in terms of being committed to political democracy, so my impression of Hong Kong as well as my impression of China reflects my bias. Quite a few years back when I was in Hong Kong, I thought the people there were only interested in money. In recent years, however, I have changed my thinking, because the people in Hong Kong, particularly students, talk in the streets in support of the democracy movement in China. They also put pressure on the Hong Kong government, and as a result, Hong Kong's governor, Christopher Patten, and others incurred the anger of Chinese authorities.

By the same token, China is changing in many ways and is becoming more like Hong Kong, but mainly superficially. Being in Guangzhou is almost like being in Hong Kong. The worship of money is now a popular practice in China, which worries me. Yes, there is an ideological vacuum in China because communism is really dead. Even some of the party cadres admit that they do not really care about communism, but that they need party membership to get into government. In the face of these developments, there has to be some commitment to the common good. Worshiping money is not enough. Fortunately, there are Chinese intellectuals who are trying to call people's attention to this—there is a commitment to society, so one should do something more than just get rich.

MR. ARMITAGE: Regarding the relation between economic reform and political reform, would it be incorrect to suggest that in southeastern China, where this rapid development is taking place, practical decisions affecting that part of the country are increasingly made locally and not in Beijing?

MR. LENG: There is a great deal of decentralization in terms of decision making both at economic and political levels. In fact, the current governor of Sichuan is a very radical person. He says that Zhao Ziyang, who was purged as a result of Tiananmen, was a good man. He talks about decision making according to local needs. As such, he is talking about pluralism mostly in economic, but also in social and political, terms. Once the mayor of Chongqing, he has been promoted to governor in spite of his radical stand. Thus, local varieties of leadership do exist as well as a discernible, though gradual, erosion of central control.

Inis L. Claude, John Armitage, and Shao-chuan Leng

I mentioned the so-called floating population. The communists at one time used the unit to which people belonged to control their lives: rations, food, and all other needs and activities. Now people do not belong to any unit, so now there are almost 100 million people moving and floating from place to place. This shift is bound to have a serious impact on social and political control, further encouraging local governments.

QUESTION: There seems to be quite a bit of attention and interest in southern China's economic growth. What about the previous growth in Manchuria?

MR. LENG: Manchuria is doing fairly well. It is now beginning to develop a little more quickly because in addition to the Chinese, the Koreans and Japanese are trying to invest there. As a result, Manchuria now has the foreign investment necessary to develop its industrial base.

NARRATOR: We are very grateful to professors Claude, Armitage, and Leng for giving us their perspectives on China in the 1990s.

87

II

JAPAN, CHINA, AND THE UNITED STATES

CHAPTER SIX

Contradictions in the Japanese-American Relationship*

CHALMERS JOHNSON

MR. LENG: Professor Chalmers Johnson is the current president of the Japan Policy Research Institute, a nonprofit research and public affairs organization devoted to public education concerning Japan. For many years he taught at the University of California campuses at Berkeley and San Diego. In fact, he played a prominent role in making Berkeley one of the leading centers of Asian studies in the world, rivaling Harvard University in the East. He has written numerous articles and reviews and several books, including *Peasant Nationalism and Communist Power: The Emergence of Revolutionary China, 1937–1945* (1962) and *MITI and the Japanese Miracle: The Growth of Industrial Policy, 1925–1975* (1982), all of which have made significant contributions to the field. In *Peasant Nationalism and Communist Power*, Professor Johnson argued that the key factor to the successful seizure of power by Chinese Communists was not their so-called social reforms, but their use of peasant nationalism against Japanese invaders. In *MITI and the Japanese Miracle*, he discusses the factors and forces behind Japan's economic development.

Presented in a Forum at the Miller Center of Public Affairs on 31 January 1995.

Professor Johnson first visited Japan in 1953 as a U.S. Navy officer and has lived and worked there virtually every year since 1961. He is currently working on a study of former Japanese Prime Minister Kakuei Tanaka and the problem of structural corruption in the Japanese state.

MR. JOHNSON: One of the institutions of the Japanese-American alliance established by the U.S.-Japan Security Treaty of 1951 is the Shimoda Conference. Shimoda is a town at the tip of the Izu Peninsula, where in 1857 Townsend Harris set up the first American consulate in Japan. Since the end of the Allied occupation of Japan after World War II, approximately 15 conferences between Japanese and Americans have been held in the otherwise unimportant, but symbolically significant, place of Shimoda, the most recent of which concluded in October 1994. In the past, Shimoda conferences have brought together a range of Japanese and American leaders from business, academics, government, and the mass media to talk about the state of the U.S.-Japan relationship. This year, reflecting the newfound and somewhat tenuous interest in the Australian-initiated Asia Pacific Economic Cooperation Forum (APEC), other Asian leaders were also invited to Shimoda. Many will recall that APEC's general meeting last year in Seattle was the occasion for the first Pacific Summit meeting. Attending Shimoda this year were representatives from South Korea, China, Indonesia, Malaysia, Thailand, Australia, Singapore, and others.

I raise this topic because what happened at Shimoda this year is an excellent example of the current central paradox of Pacific international relations. On the one hand, representatives of the APEC countries, except the United States, stressed a uniquely Asian approach to such matters as human rights, democracy, and conflict resolution. They argued that such an Asian approach includes the settlement of conflicts through consensual, collegial, and nonconfrontational norms and emphasized that these methods are preferable to the imposition of Western values on Asia—an extremely common theme these days in Asia. Events such as what happened in Waco, Texas, have only strengthened this general position. During a visit to the University of Singapore, people challenged me on the human rights question. Essentially, they said,

"We see how modern, liberal societies respond to religious dissidents. They surround them with tanks and burn them alive. Please, Professor Johnson, do not give us a lecture on human rights!" The same type of response to the United States can be found in Japan and China. The main reason people in Singapore are often more vocal about it is that they have Oxford degrees every bit as good as Bill Clinton's. In short, they speak English well and are therefore able to challenge Americans on such issues in ways that others perhaps cannot.

To return to the Shimoda Conference, Asian APEC nations also argued that they were underrepresented in the annual G-7 summit meetings of the advanced industrial democracies and that in the future they should coordinate their views with Japan prior to the G-7 summits. Their views would then be presented at the summit by Japan. When asked why the United States or Canada could not equally well represent APEC views, they answered that Japan is an Asian nation.

The paradox is that for all their talk of Asian values and consensual conflict resolution, Asian delegates to this year's Shimoda Conference also argued that a continued U.S. military presence was essential to the stability and peaceful economic development of the Western Pacific. In fact, they tended to view any U.S. military withdrawal as a potential source of uncertainty and instability in the region and as likely to result in tension between China, Japan, and the Association of Southeast Asian Nations (ASEAN). Many delegates recognized the eventual need to develop some kind of multilateral security mechanism for the Pacific, but the particular mechanism was discussed only theoretically.

Though the Shimoda Conference is technically off the record, what delegates concluded is nevertheless important. They concluded in favor of an Asia-first strategy—what the Japanese describe as the "restoration of Asia"—but also recognized that the success of such a strategy depends on the United States playing its Cold War role. The problem, however, was that no one could think of any reason why the United States should continue to do so. With respect to Japan, the United States is defending a nation to whom it is going deeply into debt, despite a quarter century of negotiating with the Japanese toward a "mutually beneficial" trading relationship. I use the words *mutually beneficial* deliberately because they are used in the opening lines of the GATT treaty. There is no "right" to international trade. International trade must be mutually beneficial or there would be no reason to engage in it. With respect to Japan, many Americans have concluded that there is nothing mutually beneficial about trading with Japan, and many have more or less given up on what they believe to be a hopeless venture.

Comments at the Shimoda Conference are not the only evidence that Japan, the economic superpower of the Pacific, is moving toward disengagement from the United States. At the very least, Japan appears to be seriously considering reorienting its foreign policy around East Asia and the United Nations. Americans need to remind themselves that Japan is indeed an economic superpower, three-fifths the size of the United States and twice the size of Germany. It is not a small country in an economic sense.

Other evidence of Japan's new orientation is its position on Malaysian Prime Minister Datuk Sri Mahathir Mohamad's East Asian Economic Caucus (EAEC), which is intended to be a counterweight to the North American Free Trade Agreement (NAFTA). Mahathir's EAEC would exclude the English-speaking nations—Australia, New Zealand, the United States, and Canada—because NAFTA excludes Asian nations. This was Mahathir's position at the Bogor Summit in Indonesia in November 1994. What is significant about this proposal with respect to Japan is that Keizai Dōyūkai, one of Japan's biggest business groups, has formally urged the government to support the EAEC.

Equally significant, in 1993 Japan's trade surplus with other countries in East Asia for the first time exceeded its trade surplus with the United States. Using its own definitions and accounting methods, during 1993 Japan had a surplus with its Asian trading partners of some U.S. $53.6 billion compared to a U.S. $50.2 billion surplus with the United States. These figures indicate that intra-Asian trade is now more important to Japan than trans-Pacific trade is. One might argue that Japan does not wish to give up the American market and that Japan faces an economic imbalance with its immediate neighbors that is potentially just as explosive as its

94

long-term structural imbalance with the United States. For those Americans who think the United States has leverage over East Asia, however, it is also worth remembering that the American market is a wasting asset. This leverage will decline within five years from now and will probably disappear within a decade.

One final indication of the new trend in Japanese thinking comes from a recent issue of *Nikkei Business*, which is the leading business magazine of Japan and is very influential. It devoted a cover story to Japan's international reorientation with an illustration of a big pendulum swinging away from the Stars and Stripes and toward China's red flag. The article contains details about the people who are helping to design an Asia-first strategy for Japan and includes members of the Ministry of Finance (MOF) as well as officials from the Ministry of International Trade and Industry (MITI).

Over the past five years since the Berlin Wall came down and the Soviet Union imploded, three main trends have emerged in trans-Pacific relations. First, Japan's main opinion leaders—bureaucrats, heads of big business, journalists, and intellectuals—have been preparing the country for the end of the Japanese-American relationship as it is presently constituted. That is not to say that they necessarily wish it to end; rather, they see it coming to an end and are trying to prepare for it.

Second, China has begun to react to Japan's enormous economic influence by balancing Japan's potential power and by exerting its own economic influence over the overseas Chinese and non-Asian investors. Finally, the third trend is the post-Cold War drift in U.S. foreign policy, a drift that reflects not only inertia in military deployments left over from the Cold War, but also in political expediency in day-to-day policy response to domestic political considerations. While these forces are working their way into the consciousness of the peoples of the Pacific region, the concrete pattern of relations boils down to one of waiting; that is, waiting for an incident that will make the intrinsic situation extrinsic. Such an incident would reveal just how much the global balance of power has shifted in favor of Asia and how little prepared the Americans are for coping with this development. In 1994 it seemed that North Korea's deployment of nuclear weapons might have been that catalytic incident. Fortunately, skillful diplomacy has diffused that crisis, though only for the time being, as many details about North Korea remain obscure.

In fact, almost any incident in the region, particularly one that leads to the loss of American lives, has the potential to challenge the entire structure of existing arrangements. Again, this situation exists because neither the Asians nor the Americans understand why the Americans are still in East Asia. This is why the shooting down of an American who drifted over the demilitarized zone between the two Koreas—the most armed border on earth—was so explosive. The United States has 37,000 frontline troops in Korea and no understanding of what they are doing there. It was an incident that should not have happened.

The shooting down of the American also reflects sea change that has occurred following the Cold War. During the Cold War every regional conflict—Korea, Afghanistan, Iran, Iraq, to name a few—was a testing ground, a form of surrogate warfare for the two superpowers. With the end of the Cold War, however, people around the world, particularly those in the United States and the rich capitalist countries of East Asia, are having great difficulty understanding how radically different the world has become.

The United States has trouble because it does not want to confront the change in the global balance of power. All conflicts are now generally regional and local with the exception of those that involve major raw materials, such as oil, or those that have great ideological implications for Americans, such as those surrounding Israel, Ireland, and South Africa. The Americans continue to fantasize about their being the lone superpower without realizing that unipolarity renders the global dimensions of strategic competition irrelevant. Current American forces and deployments are no longer appropriate for the actual military situations that may occur, and the reality with respect to the position of the United States in the international sphere is close to being one of armed impotence. Furthermore, the United States' continued assumption of a Sparta-like role as a global policeman ignores the profound shift that is underway from military to economic power. Thus, the question of whether the United States will follow the Soviet Union into geostrategic irrelevance once it has bankrupted itself is quite prominent in the minds of many Japanese. Whether the U.S. government has finally begun to notice the size of its fiscal deficits is a question prominent in American politics as well.

Meanwhile, the Japanese, more than any other power, profited from the Cold War and are delighted to see many of its arrangements perpetuated regardless of how irrelevant they may have become. They believe that their unbalanced partnership with the United States is still viable and that they can continue to behave as an export-oriented developing country even though they enjoy the largest trade surpluses ever recorded. Japan is the first country in history to produce an annual current account surplus of over $100 billion.

Before going further, let us ask ourselves whether Japan today is really committed to the so-called restoration of Asia. From one perspective, the recent enthusiasm for all things Asian in Tokyo seems to be merely another cycle of Japan's notorious ambivalence about where it belongs in the world. A historian and member of the board of the Japan Policy Research Institute (JPRI), Ivan Hall has recently outlined a sixfold cycle to describe Japan's self-perception dilemma, which was designed primarily to illustrate fads in Japanese advertising but has broader implications with respect to Japan's future place in the world.

In the first phase, Japan identifies Asia as backward and the West as advanced, just as it did shortly after the Meiji Restoration of 1868. In the second phase, Japan commits itself to emulating the West and psychologically leaving Asia. This impulse of the Japanese to emulate the West and to separate themselves from Asia produces a domestic, nationalist reaction but also condescension on the part of the Anglo-American West. This formulation is important because it brings to our attention the problem faced by Japanese liberals, which is that they are always vulnerable domestically to attack by nationalists, who accuse them of aping Britain and the United States.

In the third phase, the Japanese respond to these slights and insults by propounding a theory of Japanese uniqueness—that is, *nihonjinron*, the science of what it means to be Japanese. Every year in Japan, there are about ten best sellers on the subject. One reason for this response is that many Japanese strongly suspect that

97

they have sold their souls and that they have lost their identity. It is particularly interesting to note that in the confrontation between Western imperialism on the one hand and Japan and China on the other, Japan went in a diametrically opposite direction from China. The Japanese chose to emulate and then join their tormentors, and as a result, they are the only East Asian member of the G-7. The Japanese are incredibly wealthy, but they have a persistent identity crisis and constantly ask themselves, how much did we give up?

The Chinese, by contrast, resisted the West and staged the world's biggest revolution. They are still enormously proud of the fact that they did not emulate the West and that they threw out the Christian missionaries. China remained extremely poor, but at least the Chinese have not felt compelled to write books about what it means to be Chinese.

In phase four of Hall's cycle, many Westerners begin agreeing with the Japanese about their uniqueness—that Japanese systems of production and governance are indeed different from those that are the norm in Anglo-American textbook and that they should be treated differently from other Western nations. This phase is well illustrated in "revisionist" writings about Japan. Revisionists are those like myself who do not believe that Japan is a clone of the United States or that it is converging with the United States. Today's Japan finds itself reacting to this revisionism with talk about the restoration of Asia and with deep irritation over the Anglo-American West's pretensions with regard to Asia. This is phase five.

Finally, phase six will be Japan's genuine attempt to return to Asia and its discovery that it has been away too long, that the Asians are no more pleased with Japanese colonialism than they were with the European or American variety, and that the economic development of China might be too expensive and might not be in Japan's long-term interest either. At this point, Hall argues that the cycle starts all over again with Japan once again returning to the West. The question is whether the current Japanese rhetoric about the restoration of Asia is just another cultural cycle involving television programs on NHK about the Silk Road and Ch'in Shih Huang Ti's tombs at Xian or whether it is a more profound reflection of post-Cold War economic regionalism and will therefore

Chalmers Johnson

lead to the development of a genuine Greater East Asia Co-prosperity Sphere built on the promise of genuine prosperity, not at the point of a bayonet as in World War II. The answers to these questions are not known, but they are probably more important to the future of peace and stability in the Pacific than any commitment the United States might make.

The most important fact about the post-Cold War Asia-Pacific region is Japan's growing economic dominance and the degree to which this is integrating the nations of the region. The means of integration are trade, direct investment, aid, financial services, technology transfer, and the consideration of Japan as an inspiration for an Asian model of development. Generally speaking, all of the Asian nations—particularly China—depend on Japan for loans, technology, investment, and foreign aid. They depend on the United States, though, to be the military counterweight to Japan and China, the market for consumer goods manufactured in Asia, and oddly but interestingly, for its higher education.

On this last point, the elites of Asia know that American universities are fabulous. As a result, they still send their young adults to America for university and graduate school. They do not send them here for grades K through 12, which illustrates one of the great asymmetries between Japan and the United States. Japan does an absolutely brilliant job educating its youths at levels K through 12, which is why Japan produces the world's most competent labor force. The Japanese, however, fall down badly at the university level, and graduate school is a farce. Westerners who talk about Japanese workaholics have never been to a Japanese university because that is where one finds the most extraordinary goof-offs ever seen on earth. The obverse is the United States. For all of its democratic pretensions, the United States does a rotten job of educating citizens. U.S. universities and graduate schools, however, are the envy of the rest of the world.

Questions to be considered concerning the Japanese-American relationship are: Can it be rebuilt along new lines? Can the celebrated hopes of APEC for free trade by 2020 be politically realized? Is the post-Cold War world to be divided into three blocks—a "G-3," made up of Europe, North America, and Asia, with Japan as its leader? Europe is a fact, so the only real question left

99

is, Will it be a G-2 or G-3 future? That is, will Japan and the United States be allies, or will Japan and the United States tend to their own particular regions? The tendency is certainly toward regions and a G-3 future.

In my opinion, the historic contribution of the United States to the enrichment of Asia was not particularly its military deployments, diplomacy, or treaties. It was its markets. The United States bought the high-quality, low-priced manufactured goods first from Japan, then from the so-called NICs (newly industrialized countries)—South Korea, Taiwan, Hong Kong, and Singapore—then from Southeast Asia, and today from mainland China. Without a market for these products, there would be no East Asian economic miracle. One problem has always been Japan's comparison of the East Asian economies to a V-formation of flying geese with Japan always as head-goose—never mind the obvious problem that China does not like being number-two goose in anything and never will like flying behind Japan. The general problem, however, is that no one ever asked where these geese were flying. Up to now, they have been flying to Los Angeles, but in the post-Cold War era, the United States can no longer play its traditional role. A new primary market for Asian manufactured goods must be found. Moreover, the center of global manufacturing gravity has shifted from Europe and North America to an area stretching from Tokyo to Singapore. Nothing else matches it, and that is not likely to change. Hence, Japan will have to become the new market, or the Asia-Pacific region will experience serious economic instability in the years to come.

As Americans, we are all thoroughly and perpetually indoctrinated by the editorial pages of the *Wall Street Journal* and London's *Economist* with the idea that GATT has something to do with free trade and is a free trade doctrine. GATT, however, can be easily understood without any reference to economics at all. It can just as easily be understood as a grand strategy pursued by the United States against the Soviet Union, in which the United States offered to nations such as Japan a trade-off: unlimited access to the U.S. market in return for basing rights and votes in the United Nations. Hence, GATT has been in trouble since the day the Cold War ended. GATT can be rewritten into becoming the World Trade

Organization (WTO), but the fact that GATT/WTO is no longer as viable as it once was will not change.

The American market is not shutting down because of policy decisions. Neither is it closing down completely. Nevertheless, the American market can no longer play its traditional Cold War role for at least four reasons. First, the American economy is not growing fast enough to absorb most of Asia's exports, as it did during the Cold War. The United States would not want it to grow that fast because if it did, the environmental damage alone would be enormous. Second, the produce of Asia is now so large that no distant foreign market could possibly absorb it all. Third, the United States needs to cut consumption as a percentage of GDP and increase its savings and investment. By contrast, Japan needs to do the opposite and increase consumption. Consumption in the United States today constitutes fully 68 percent of the domestic economy, whereas it is only about 56 percent in Japan. The Americans for all intents and purposes save nothing and consume everything. The Japanese, on the other hand, save quite a bit, which gives them a great deal of leverage in this world. The Japanese are right to say that Americans consume too much, and one of the best things to cut down on would be Japanese imports. That would be a good and logical thing for the U.S. government to do.

Fourth, the United States has no alternative but to tend to the demographic and socioeconomic trends taking place among its southern neighbors, particularly Mexico. To do otherwise would be to leave open the possibility that what happened in Nicaragua during the 1980s will occur along the entire length of the U.S. southern border. The answer that the United States has proposed is to give Mexico privileged access to its market, which implies some closure of the American market to Japanese platforms in Malaysia and elsewhere in Southeast Asia, just as Prime Minister Mahathir suspected. In my view, his proposed EAEC was as much intended to pressure Japan to open its markets as it was aimed at the United States for giving preference to Latin America.

The United States is very much aware of the importance of its military forces in East Asia. The United States is virtually the only Pacific power with the capacity to project power over long distances.

That role should not be abandoned, but it needs to be based on a realistic post-Cold War policy toward Asia.

The United States no longer has any need to intervene in a Korean civil war-type conflict. Its presence in the Korean War four decades ago was dictated by concern for the actions of Communist China and the Soviet Union. Today these nations—China and Russia—have diplomatic relations with the country they were then fighting. Americans do not really know what 37,000 front-line U.S. troops are doing in Korea any more. Moreover, the Republic of Korea has two times the population and ten times the productive power of North Korea. It should be fully capable of defending itself in any contest that did not involve external powers or nuclear weapons. The United States should continue to guarantee the Republic of Korea security from nuclear attack, but American ground forces that have been based in the country for almost 50 years should be withdrawn. Many analysts agree with this argument, but they always add that the time is not appropriate. They fail to note that there will never be a perfect time and that leaving American troops in Korea makes them hostage to possible events over which the United States has no control. The unification of Korea is a topic for Korean politics. The United States can help, but it should not be in the middle of the situation.

Similarly, the United States no longer has any reason to support the politically conservative Liberal Democratic Party (LDP) in Japan just because it is anti-Communist, as the CIA did from 1955 to 1972. The long era of LDP dominance is one of the main issues preoccupying Japanese politics at the present time. The Japanese ask why they do not have a two-party system as Germany does, and some Japanese are answering that they might have had a viable two-party system if the Americans had not embraced the LDP quite so warmly in the 1960s.

The United States has every reason to promote multiparty democracy in Japan. If that means the United States must force the *zaikai*—the business community in Japan—to liberalize by pressuring them with the high-yen, retaliatory trade actions and managed trade, then that is what should be done. Incidentally, if and when Japan does liberalize economically and politically, the United States will not be the chief beneficiary. Rather, the rest of Asia and Australia are the ones that stand to gain the most.

The most important new element in the Asia-Pacific region is a China growing at double-digit rates. For a long time, the Chinese Communists refused to heed the lessons of high-growth, capitalist Asia. These lessons are that state-guided capitalism could use the market for developmental purposes and produce results undreamed of in either socialist or laissez-faire economics. That is why the Japanese are challenging us. Amaya Naohiro, the former chief strategist at the Ministry of International Trade and Industry (MITI) once told me that his ministry had discovered a correlation between the number of Americans winning the Nobel Prize in economics and the decline of the American economy. He said he would be truly alarmed should a Japanese ever win the Nobel Prize in economics, as it correlates so perfectly with economic incompetence. Moreover, based on evidence from East Asia today, at least two Nobel Prizes in economics held by Americans should be given back because they were wrong. (Since they were in economics, they should probably be given back with interest.) It is this challenge from Japan that particularly bothers people because it strongly suggests that Americans, particularly economists, did not anticipate great wealth in East Asia. We Americans still cannot explain Japan's success in ways that are consistent with the theories taught in our economics courses, and we are enormously threatened by it intellectually. According to our theories, Asia should be headed toward Brezhnev's Russia, but it is not. Note the difference, however, between the socialist displacement of the market and the use of the market for developmental purposes—that is, the state's support of the market to achieve national goals. Asia's success is based on the latter.

The Chinese Communists at first refused to follow Japan's example. They feared that the American propagandists were right and that reliance on market forces would eventually undercut the Communist regime politically and lead to some form of democratization. By the time of the 14th Party Congress in 1992, however, the Chinese Communists had concluded that the Americans were wrong. High growth Asian countries, Singapore in particular, had achieved high levels of per capita income with little or no real pressure to change politically. The Chinese, therefore, committed themselves to the use of their market for developmental purposes and started to grow at a rate of 10 to 12 percent per annum. Now, they are the fastest growing economy on earth, and since they also happen to be the world's largest social system, these are big changes.

China explains its new development strategy in terms of its adherence to Asian values, by which it means the combining of market forces and the promise of private wealth with a hard-as-nails authoritarian government. There is neither a pretense of democracy nor even a bowing in the direction of it in China. Today the results are there for all to see: high growth, cheap docile labor (often female and thoroughly exploited), high returns on investment, human rights abuses, and the use of a prison gulag to produce export products. The United States has not improved this situation with its human rights rhetoric, and whether high-speed economic growth will actually help or hinder political development in China is a distinctly open question.

When the world's largest social system begins to grow as fast as it is growing today, it also rapidly alters both the regional and the world balance of power. In a short time China may have an economy as big or bigger than that of the United States, but with a per capita income still only one-fourth to one-sixth that of the United States. When such economic power is combined with China's thermonuclear capabilities, its continued nuclear testing, its scheduled absorption of Hong Kong in 1997, its growing economic community of interest with Russia (China has moved from being Russia's 17th largest trading partner before the onset of perestroika to second place today, just behind Germany), its cultivation of the overseas Chinese as investors and as potential members of a "greater China," one has a right to be concerned. How should other Asian nations and the world at large react to the emergence of China as a potential superpower in every sense of the term?

Japan's response thus far has been to do everything in its power to adjust to China. Japan's current policy of "adjusting" is at the very core of its so-called strategy of restoring Asia. So far this strategy has included a visit by the Japanese emperor to China. This event may not seem important to Americans, but it was significant for the Japanese and was also quite controversial. Other elements of Japan's strategy include: formal apologies in the Diet from former Prime Minister Hosokawa and others for Japanese atrocities committed in China during World War II; loans from the Industrial Bank of Japan to China that are extended to no other country; a stance on human rights that varies from soft to nonexistent; aid-trade technology transfer and direct investment on the highest priority basis. Japan is also tolerating without a murmur China's criticism of Japan's various contacts with Taiwan—from the Asia Games to the Asian Development Bank, even though the Taiwanese remain the only people in Asia with a long record of truly liking the Japanese.

Japan's strategy may even work. The Chinese and the Japanese are enjoying a flourishing commerce, which has the potential of growing into a community of interest that could lead to more formal cooperation in the future—and this potential cannot be underestimated. Americans have a tendency to believe that China and Japan will continue to dislike each other and that the United States can depend on that fact. It is not at all clear that this assumption is true. It is rather like the relationship between the United States and England. In the 19th century, one would have thought they would have been perpetual enemies. Now there are probably more supporters of the House of Windsor in Virginia than there are in England.

At the same time, it is clear that the Japanese are betting a lot on *jingji zhuyi*, which means economism. Japan is hoping that the creation of strong ties between China, Japan, and other East Asian capitalist markets will produce a more predictable and less antagonistic foreign policy based on economic considerations. Unfortunately, the Chinese have a long record of pursuing political goals regardless of the economic consequences. China's conduct of its relations with Britain over Hong Kong is but one example. This is what makes the Japanese strategy so risky. Again, what is written in the financial press is misleading. Hong Kong is booming, of course, but it is booming with people who have passports—people who know that if things in Hong Kong do not work out, they can move to Brisbane, Melbourne, or Vancouver. China wants Hong Kong back, but only on its own terms. Whether China has overestimated its ability to digest Hong Kong, however, is another question entirely.

Indeed, the weak foundations of China's current development strategy and its possible consequences raise many questions. From Beijing, repeated warnings are made about the lack of a pilot agency. There is no MITI-type agency to guide China's high-speed economic growth as there was in Japan. There are also warnings about structural corruption, the loss of morality in public affairs, severe center-periphery conflicts, restiveness on the part of the army, the dangers of lifting the controls on internal travel, and certainly, endless talk about what will happen after Deng Xiaoping finally, as the Chinese press puts it, "goes to meet Marx." On this last point, the most immediate consequence of Deng's death will be a return to tight authoritarian controls and a crackdown on corruption, all justified by the new popularity of Asian values. If a severe crackdown occurs and is linked to so-called Asian values, it will test Japan's ability to remain friends with both the United States and China.

As the world witnesses the shift from the "enrichment" to the "empowerment" of East Asia, the most important relationship will be that between China and Japan. How it will develop remains to be seen, but if Japan's current efforts to cultivate China fail, then there is a role for the United States to play in East Asia. In such a case, the United States will need to use its power to forge and maintain a balance of power. The idea of balancing power in Asia is controversial, as it opens up questions about who will be the major players in East Asia and whose relations would need to be kept in balance. Some analysts include Russia and India on that list, but both are likely to be too internally preoccupied to play a major role in international relations. Instead, the balance of power in East Asia will require a balance among China, Japan, and ASEAN, with a unified Korea and Vietnam playing the most important buffer roles much as Poland and Belgium did in Europe after the Congress of Vienna. The United States would play the role of external balancer, guaranteeing the security of Korea and Vietnam by shifting its support among the major powers in order to maintain a balance. This portrayal is a realistic formulation of East Asia's future balance of power, but I find that few Americans have much stomach for it. When the idea that the United States might guarantee the security of Vietnam against China was raised in Washington recently, the reaction was, "Why don't we instead adjust to and cooperate with China?" Such a reaction ignores the political realities in East Asia.

People in the United States know that their last three major wars began in Asia. The United States, however, only won one of those wars. Americans did not win the Korean War, and they were thrown out of Vietnam. Nonetheless, history offers us every reason to continue playing a constructive role in maintaining the security of the Asia-Pacific region. That role includes the deployment and use of U.S. military forces, particularly the highly visible U.S. carrier task forces, in ways that would be supported in Asia. At the same time, the United States has no reason to try to balance the power of Japan and China without also acquiring a major stake in the extraordinary economic prosperity of East Asia. As it stands today, American troops based in Japan cannot even afford to leave their bases for a bowl of noodles given the yen-dollar exchange rate.

At Shimoda, several Asian participants asked the Americans, "What is your price to stay in Asia militarily?" That question, it seems to me, is exactly the one that should be asked and answered. Unfortunately, even if an agreement on a new role for the United States in Asia could be reached, no one knows if the American people will want to play it—regardless of what history teaches. The situation cries out for innovative political leadership of at least the Marshall Plan variety.

In summary, the current relationship between the United States and Japan is unstable, regardless of what American political or military leaders may say. The Japanese-American alliance lasted from approximately 1950 to 1990 and was based on Cold War concerns. With the Cold War over, the old relationship between Japan and the United States is now characterized by inertia. U.S.-Japan relations are now waiting to be given a new foundation or for some incident to reveal that the old relations are moribund. The Cold War is over, but it is not the end of history, regardless of what Francis Fukuyama and others might say. It is more a time of history restarted, which means that all countries should be open to a range of contingencies—and they should also keep their powder dry.

QUESTION: What are your thoughts about the Japanese reaction to the recent Kobe earthquake?

MR. JOHNSON: JPRI is currently working on a special project on this subject. The Kobe earthquake was Japan's wake-up call. Indeed, it may be as important for Japan as the collapse of the Berlin Wall was for Eastern Europe. The Japanese have had a deep interest in the Cold War system and have tended to want to perpetuate it as long as possible. Japanese attitudes toward the Americans have been, "Don't ask us to change. We adjusted to the world created by you, the conquerors. We don't mind if you continue to throw your weight around, even if you have to borrow our money to do it. Indeed, it serves our interests."

The Japanese are right. The Cold War arrangement has served Japanese interests extremely well. One notes, for example, that Japan is more dependent on Persian Gulf oil than any other nation, yet Japan did not participate in the Gulf War. Instead, it paid for it. Japan paid $13 billion to send General Norman Schwarzkopf and 500,000 other Americans to the Persian Gulf.

The Kobe earthquake is significant because it highlighted the weaknesses of the Japanese government through the suffering of the earthquake's victims. The earthquake may thus bring to an end Japan's "dollar diplomacy." Consider, for example, that the magnitude of the Kobe earthquake was about the same as that of the Northridge earthquake in Southern California. Less than 100 people died in Northridge, but some 5,000 died in Kobe. As a result, this incident raises some very serious, but salutary, questions for the Japanese public about the performance of their own government. The Kobe earthquake suggests to the Japanese public that although Japan is the main source of long-term capital on earth today, it may no longer be a good idea to continue lending its money to over-consuming, rich Americans, Mexicans, or even potentially deserving Chinese. The Japanese can better use the money at home. One certain consequence of such a conclusion would be a rise in the cost of capital. The United States would have pay more to use someone else's savings.

A member of the board of the JPRI, Robert "Skipp" Orr of Nippon Motorola, holds a doctorate in politics, is perfectly fluent in Japanese, and has lived in Japan most of his life. When the earthquake occurred, he decided that Motorola would give away free cellular phones to the people of Kobe. Over the objections of the Japanese government, Orr and his staff took some phones, rode the train as far as they could, bicycled their way into the most devastated area of Kobe, and gave away telephones. His plan worked well, even though some Japanese later accused Motorola of trying to profit from the tragedy. Most ordinary people, though, welcomed him, and he was touched to walk into a refugee center and hear an old woman exclaim in Japanese, "Ah, the Americans have come! Now we're saved!" It was just like the end of the war—they were going to get hot soup and a decent blanket after all.

Orr's experience also illustrates how the Japanese, just like the Americans, have avoided seeing how the world has changed. The old world was characterized by an artificial, unimaginable peace in which two old leaders—Reagan and Brezhnev—pretended to threaten each other. With the Cold War over, the world has become a more dangerous, unpredictable place.

QUESTION: In your talk, you made the assumption that the United States will continue to maintain a military presence in Asia so that it can balance China or Japan against each other or from Southeast Asia, assuming a continued American interest in the stability of the region. In an age in which U.S. citizens do not like to see 20 Americans killed in a far-off part of the world, is it not possible that we will oppose the stationing of fleet units in Asia to perform this function if it costs lives and money?

MR. JOHNSON: Yes. This dilemma is exactly what I am trying to explain. To a certain extent, the Japanese have the United States boxed in. The United States protects them, but at the same time Americans are scared to death of letting the Japanese defend themselves. It reminds me of something the late Ambassador Reischauer once said to me: "You talk about burden-sharing.

Name me a burden that you want to put down that you really want the Japanese to take up." His argument was that the true payoff in the victory of 1945 has been a disarmed Japan. To a certain extent, this is also Japan's blackmail. The United States can send troops home if it wants, Japan argues, but regional instability may follow.

The fact of the matter is that a U.S. role in East Asia, if clearly thought through, does serve a purpose. The danger is in failing to plan, which is why the United States has continued to act out its old role. Meanwhile, Japan figures that the United States is in a kind of Roman phase. The United States might have to borrow the money to do it, but it still enjoys throwing its weight around. Therefore, the United States has been allowed to continue playing its old role. As a result, there is too great a danger for U.S. foreign policy to drift—that is, until some incident catalyzes these relationships and produces a severe reaction on the part of the American public.

Americans are not without historical knowledge. Those families that have had loved ones killed in warfare. They most likely lost them in Vietnam or Korea. The United States still has an interest in maintaining stability in the Pacific. Consider also that California is an unimaginably important part of the Pacific Rim. The largest trade flows on earth, other than those across the Canadian border, are between East Asia and California. I think that the question of U.S. commitments abroad is an issue of the times, but I also believe that in the long run, the United States has a valuable role to play in East Asia. It will require, however, a rethinking of U.S. strategy, and this new strategy should be one of much greater flexibility and maneuver. It will probably involve fewer ground-based forces based, as these bases are not of any great long-term importance.

Despite the endless complaints from the Pentagon about what would happen if the United States closed Clark Field and Subic Bay—the two largest military installations outside of the United States—in the end, Mount Pinatubo closed down one for us and the Philippine senate closed the other, and no one noticed. One place is now covered with volcanic ash, and the other is just padlocked. The quiet passing of these two bases shows that it is not at all clear that the old Cold War relationships are necessary even for stability,

110

though one should note that many Asians *think* they are. The press reports from Asia make it quite clear that the Asians do not want the Americans to go home.

One reason that the Korean nuclear issue is so significant is that it has the potential to set off nuclear proliferation in both South Korea and Japan. Japan is a country that has proliferated without testing, and as a result, Japan's stockpiling of plutonium is very important. If Japan were to decide to become a nuclear power, it might take a full afternoon to do it; Japan is more than technologically capable of becoming a nuclear power.

In a sense, North Korea's attempt at nuclear diplomacy was brilliant. North Korea is a little country that lost the Cold War. It is isolated, driven into a corner, and treated with contempt by the Americans. The North Koreans asked themselves how they might capture the attention of the United States, and they concluded, "Atomic bombs!" After all, the United States has not made it easy for the losers in the Cold War. The remaining Kim Il Sungs and Fidel Castros of the world are well aware that Ceausescu was put up against the wall and shot and that the leaders of East Germany are being tried and convicted. Under these circumstances, North Korea was truly brilliant in capturing the attention of the United States.

Public sentiment in the United States also helped North Korea. Earlier in 1994, the U.S. government had been filled with supporters of surgical strikes to prevent nuclear proliferation. Only ever so slowly did some Korean specialists begin to convince these hawks that any use of force in Korea would have negative effects. In the end, the politicians also reminded them that all it would take would be one American killed for the American public to rise up in response. North Korea illustrates how insecure the American military is about how far-off it can use American forces and how many casualties in East Asia Americans are willing to accept, and Asians are aware of this insecurity.

As for Kim Il Sung, he basically did not want to go to his grave known as the Stalin of the North. Moreover, like Mao Zedong in 1972, Kim wanted some acknowledgment of his legitimacy. The difference, however, is that whereas the Chinese revolution was indeed legitimate, the Korean War was both a civil war and a

Communist aggression. Therefore, the United States could not meet Kim Il Sung and offer him what he wanted the way that Nixon did Mao. Jimmy Carter's visit, though, in the end proved to be the functional equivalent of Nixon's visit to China. The U.S. government should have tried Carter and negotiations with North Korea a long time ago.

QUESTION: Are you suggesting that China will be the major threat to the balance of power in East Asia and Southeast Asia and that the United States should follow a policy of restricting China?

MR. JOHNSON: I specifically do not wish to take that position. My point is that the United States should be prepared to play the role of a neutral balancer in East Asia. If Japan were menacing the stability of the area, the United States should be prepared to side with China and ASEAN. Similarly, if China were the menacing power, the United States should be prepared to side with Japan and ASEAN. My point is not that China should be singled out. In fact, there remains a great deal of goodwill toward China in the United States, which terrifies the Japanese. From the Japanese point of view, the worst possible situation would be one in which the Chinese and the Americans start liking each other again, as they did in World War II. The Japanese really do not want that to happen.

On the other hand, the Chinese are alarmed by the post-Cold War continuation of the Japanese-American alliance. It may have made some sense while the Soviet Union was still a potent force, but today it looks more like a new form of hegemony. China's claim to all of the South China Sea as territorial waters might be seen as one example of its resistance to such an arrangement, and China's actions are, in turn, disturbing to Japan and Southeast Asia. Since Japan's oil must travel through the South China Sea, however, Japan keeps quiet about the situation, especially since China is a considerably more formidable military power than Japan is.

My point is not to identify an enemy. Rather, I want to emphasize that the United States needs to recognize that Asia is returning to a more complex set of relations that the Cold War had superseded. The Cold War is but a short period in a history of world politics that is two millennia old. The study of economics, which is only two centuries old, is also brief when compared to the study of world politics and conflict causation. In East Asia, many different nations are on collision courses, but the identification of a collision course does not mean that collision is inevitable. If the United States does not want a collision with China or Japan, it needs a change of course, and it had better start staffing the government with people who know something about these places.

NARRATOR: Thank you for a very thought-provoking presentation of current Japanese-U.S. relations and what course they may take in the future.

CHAPTER SEVEN

Japan's Reforms and Relations with America*

STEPHEN J. ANDERSON

NARRATOR: Professor Shao-chuan Leng, who is the head of the Miller Center's Asian political leadership program, will introduce our speaker.

MR. LENG: Professor Anderson received his bachelor's degree from Oberlin College and his master's and doctorate degrees from MIT. He is a specialist on Japan and the Pacific Basin. He has taught at the University of Wisconsin and the International University of Japan and is currently teaching courses on Japan in the Department of Government and Foreign Affairs at the University of Virginia. Professor Anderson received impressive grants from the Japan Foundation and Fulbright Program for language training and field research. He is the author of a well-received book, *Welfare Politics and Policy in Japan: Beyond the Developmental State* (1993). We are fortunate to have Professor Anderson here to speak on Japan's reforms and relations with America.

Presented in a Forum at the Miller Center of Public Affairs on 10 February 1994.

MR. ANDERSON: Japan's policymakers are facing both domestic economic reforms and changes in Japan's relations with America. To give you an idea of these bureaucrats studied in depth by Chalmers Johnson, I would like to recite his version of the light-bulb joke: How many neoclassical liberal economists does it take to screw in a light bulb? The answer, of course, is none; they wait for the "invisible hand" to screw in the bulb.

Japanese policymakers are well versed in American economics—the Chicago School with Milton Friedman and Harvard with Jeffrey Sachs. They have an understanding of liberal economists and neoclassical liberal economics. I do not believe that the policymakers have much faith in the invisible hand, however, especially given Japan's guided recovery in the postwar era by the Ministry of International Trade and Industry (MITI) and by their effective interventionist industrial policy. The Ministry of Finance (MOF) could also be added to this list, as its control over foreign investment and foreign exchange laws ensures that a tight set of plans can be adjusted easily without fear of a rapid or deep disruption of Japan's political economy.

I propose to discuss three areas of reform in Japan and three issues in its relations with America. In the area of reforms, I will consider deregulation, the election system, and a recently announced tax-cut stimulus package. With regard to Japan's relations with America, I will evaluate Prime Minister Hosokawa's personal relations with President Clinton and U.S. diplomats, U.S.-Japanese security relations, and the economic trade relations between the two countries.

As a prelude to these comments, I offer a brief review of Japanese politics. On 18 June 1993, the Liberal Democratic Party (LDP), which has governed the regime in Japan since 1955 and was instrumental in Japan's economic recovery, suddenly faced a profound crisis that eventually ended its term in power. Through a vote of no-confidence in the Diet in June, the Liberal Democrats under Prime Minister Kiichi Miyazawa, had to change their leadership, and in doing so, they lost control of the government. They called a snap election a month later on 18 July 1993, which confirmed that they had lost their majority in the Lower House.

The leadership of the party made Yohei Kono, a former rebel from the party, their leader, but the LDP is now an opposition party.

It is a striking change. The people who were once assured of a fast track to power, roles in the cabinet, and possibly the prime ministership now have careers that are in disarray. It is not clear whether Kono will have much influence except as an opposition leader. This change occurred because challengers and rebels in the party led a revolt. The revolt's most prominent head, Tsutomu Hata, is now the foreign minister and is also acting as deputy prime minister. Hata was part of a group of reformers in the party who felt that the Liberal Democrats should not stay in power. He was teamed with an important strategist, Ichiro Ozawa, who pulled the necessary strings to form the group which felt that the scandal-ridden LDP needed to reform itself. In the face of the revolt, Ozawa was tainted with scandal and as a result remains in the background, but he is still a key figure in Japanese politics and in Japan's future.

Other opposition groups in Japan include the Japan Socialist Party (JSP)—or as they call themselves now, the Social Democratic Party—who for the longest time were not able to seize power, except for one brief period after the war. The Socialists lost so many seats in the 1993 election that they are no longer considered a serious opposition party. Quantitatively, they are still the largest member party of the coalition, but I believe they are going to face further splits and be removed from the scene as a viable opposition party.

The labor unions will be the real power of the Left in Japan in the future. The labor unions, under the leadership of Akina Yamagishi, remained a critical component in the formation of the coalition after the 1993 election. They were the ones who brought all of the other parties to the table. Thus, these unions with their fairly new federation, having been brought together over team labor splits, will be key players in the coalition governments of the future. They were able to bring together various groups in opposition to the past government and to form a coalition under the leadership of Morihiro Hosokawa, the prime minister, whom many people felt was merely a figurehead leader at the time.

Hosokawa's role in terms of national politics was extremely new. He was elected to the Upper House less than a year before

117

he became prime minister. Then in the July election he was elected to the more powerful Lower House for the first time. Hosokawa, as a reform figure, happened to be in the right place at the right time. He was aided and assisted by the chief of staff, Masayoshi Takemura, a Liberal Democratic politician and a key figure in his organization. Thus, the role of the chief of staff in Hosokawa's regime under Takemura is extremely important for understanding how Japanese politics operates.

To recap my comments on these issues, the Liberal Democrats are out, and their leader, Kono, must appeal to the media to be successful. The members of the Liberal Democrats who led the revolt, Hata and Ozawa, are extremely important because of their positions in the cabinet. Hata is the foreign minister and Ozawa is in the background still trying to pull the strings. I do not believe the Socialists in this coalition, however, will be very influential except in dealing with the labor unions, although they have seemed important in the news recently. The labor unions, of course, are influential in funding and supporting future coalitions. Finally, the current prime minister, Hosokawa, is very much dependent on his chief of staff in determining a strategy. It is difficult to see him as a strong political figure whose influence will continue over a long period of time.

With the new prime minister, many difficulties exist in Japanese politics. Prime Minister Hosokawa did come in and say that he wanted to push through major reforms in Japanese politics, the cornerstone of which was deregulation. To deregulate, Hosokawa had to oppose the bureaucrats—MITI and MOF—and the policymakers who led the economic recovery while at the same time wresting control from other key Japanese political figures.

One of the most visible components in deregulation was the rice import issue. The price control system for rice has been extremely important for the Ministry of Agriculture and their dealings with the countryside throughout Japan. By introducing rice imports, Hosokawa and his administration will always be remembered as an administration that initiated some important changes.

It was announced on 8 February 1994 that a ministry had discussed medium-term administrative reform in 1,591 areas—a huge number—over the next five years. This plan raises some critical points, particularly for issues such as automobile inspections. If the automobile inspection system is changed, consumers in Japan will no longer be forced to buy new automobiles year in and year out. This regulation is an indirect means of subsidizing the Japanese automobile industry because manufacturers are able to count on people buying new automobiles regularly. Thus, that type of policy might be an effective deregulatory measure. Other changes in the distribution system and in telecommunication systems might also be helpful in promoting deregulatory matters. All of these areas and others are on the list. It is important to keep in mind that it is a five-year plan; therefore, none of these things will be deregulated tomorrow. Looking at the timetable, however, my conclusion is that progress in deregulation so far has not been substantial. While the discussions provide hope, Hosokawa has not had great success in changing those areas that are the cornerstones of his deregulation program.

The reform of the election system was the key issue that brought the coalition together in the first place. Another long-term problem for the Liberal Democrats has been the scandals that occurred regularly during their time in office. In the cycle of scandals, however, the LDP had always been able to reprimand offenders with a slap on the wrist and then send them out to do public service work—not in leadership roles, of course—and then rehabilitate them as the pressure of public opinion declined. This approach changed last summer when Hata and Ozawa decided to split with the party. When they left the Liberal Democrats, they made the issue of scandal the reason for their split. Ozawa, while he might have been tainted by his close association with key figures in past scandals, turned this connection into an asset by saying that he supported reform of the political system in Japan. Prime Minister Hosokawa and other people in the coalition agreed that Japan needed a way to reform both politics and their election system.

The Japanese public was confused because the people thought that the political system was going to be reformed and that politicians would not get kickbacks. They also thought the funding system would change and there would be a way to deal with that issue. But, the only important reform for politicians was election reform. They felt that the root cause of their problems was the rules of the games, themselves, and how people were elected. Political reform was not a matter of money reform, even though that statement was made in the press. In the Japanese system, established 70 years ago before the current Japanese Constitution and the American occupation, three to six members were elected from each district, not just one member from each district, as is the case in Britain and the United States. As part of the recent reforms, politicians decided to introduce the single-member election district. Rather than deal with the money issue, they wanted to deal with how people are elected.

In the beginning of the prime minister's time in office, this issue of election reform rose to the top of the agenda. It became the only item on which the coalition could agree. To the public's surprise in November, the prime minister succeeded in forcing through a bill that would change the system. In January, the bill encountered difficulty in the Upper House of the Japanese Diet, which is unusual, since the coalition had a majority. People thought it would easily pass. On 21 January 1994, in a vote of 130 to 118, however, the prime minister was unable to force the reform bill through the Upper House. Many people took Hosokawa's inability to pass election reform as a sign of crisis in Japanese politics. In an 11th-hour deal between the opposition and the LDP's Kono, a major reform of the rules of the electoral system was passed with a significant amendment to the initial proposal.

It was agreed that in the future the Lower House of Japan's Diet would be elected on the basis of 300 new single-member election districts where lines had never been drawn before. Two hundred additional Diet members would be elected under proportional representation, so that the parties could run an additional set of candidates under proportional representation, which would occur in only 11 districts, not nationwide. As a result, the next Diet in Japan will be elected under entirely new rules. Thus, the current Diet is a lame duck; they will have to abide by this new election reform implemented on Christmas Day 1994.

The details of this election reform in Japan have yet to be decided. It will be the only thing about which the politicians in

Stephen J. Anderson

Japan will be concerned, as they probably will not be able to deal with anything else. In considering Japanese relations with America, people should realize that the Japanese politicians' hands will be tied.

Japanese politicians were, however, able to pass a set of policy measures designed to address the structural stagnation of Japan's economy. Last week, they passed a tax-cut and stimulus public works package. This package is going to mean a 5.47 trillion yen— which is about U.S. $50 billion—income tax cut. That is an interesting number. If they could just take that income tax cut and make Japanese consumers buy only American products, then we would have a trade balance between our two countries; obviously, that is not likely to happen. Policymakers did pass another $90 billion—9.78 trillion yen—stimulus package of public works programs, which makes the total package equivalent to a $140-billion jump start to their $2 trillion economy. Prime Minister Hosokawa took a real beating on his proposal because initially he said he would pay for it by more than doubling the consumption—the indirect sales—tax in Japan. He had to drop that provision in order to pass his proposal. As a result, they have no plan to pay for this. It really is a purely Keynesian means of jump starting the economy.

The reaction to the new tax-and-spend policies has been mixed. The manipulator, Ozawa, quipped to the press that he did not think the Japanese consumers were going to buy more products. He thought that they would save half of the tax cuts and thus make the stimulus package less effective. U.S. Treasury Secretary Lloyd Bentsen agreed, saying that the huge $140 million package was modest. I think that despite the lack of growth over the past year, this program, given the basic strength of Japan's large corporations and Japan's long-term plans for economic growth, is a good one. Unemployment in Japan has increased from 2.8 to 2.9 percent, but Japan's economy, nevertheless, remains basically sound.

What do all of these changes mean for Japan's relations with America? First, Bill Clinton really liked Hosokawa when he first met him. Clinton took a chance by meeting Prime Minister Hosokawa and the foreign minister, Deputy Prime Minister Hata, at a reception hosted by the savvy diplomats at the U.S. Embassy during the July 1993 summit, which was before the new coalition was even elected. Clinton's move scandalized the Liberal Democratic Party, which felt that Clinton was interfering in domestic politics. Nevertheless, it was clever, because when Hosokawa became prime minister, he had already met Clinton. Consequently, when they met again in Seattle and at later stages, there were photo opportunities for the two "agents of change"—that is, change and reform in Japan and change and reform in the United States. Both were able to use media events to show that they had established some type of relationship.

Remember that Hosokawa is Clinton's Yeltsin in Japan in that Clinton can draw upon him for the political leverage needed to encourage change in Japan and to encourage better relations between the United States and Japan. The analogy is useful, but it is also limited. Clinton has alternatives that are possibly just as good as Hosokawa with regard to change and reform in U.S.-Japan relations. Such alternatives are not available with regard to Russia.

Clinton is in fact fortunate to have alternatives because Hosokawa is in trouble. Hosokawa's original popularity rating of 70 percent is now down to about 52 percent. Moreover, as a result of his personal friendship with the key figure in the package express company scandal, Hosokawa was recently linked for the first time to the very scandals that brought down the LDP last summer. Hosokawa, like the current Diet, may be seen as a lame duck prime minister once the election reforms are finalized. People like Hata and Ozawa are going to be very eager for an election, not to mention the Liberal Democrats who have been out of power and were always expected to be in power.

In terms of U.S.-Japan security issues, the North Korean situation threatens to become extremely difficult for Japan and is likely to affect U.S.-Japan relations. Ozawa has said that he believes North Korea already has a nuclear weapon. If North Korea does have one, it would be able to use it on their No Dong I missiles, which is an intermediate-range missile. The North Koreans have already shown that they can successfully launch it into the Sea of Japan and hit Osaka and possibly Tokyo.

The solution suggested by Ozawa is a collective security arrangement that would be the equivalent of NATO in Asia. The head of the Komei Party, an Ozawa supporter, agrees that a collective security arrangement ought to be established. Though Ozawa and the coalition are still officially supportive of the U.S.-Japan Security Treaty and their proposal does not reflect a credible desire to change that in the short term, Ozawa's suggestion implies that Japan wants to change the U.S.-Japan security arrangement in the medium to long term. The U.S.-Japan Security Treaty is critical in that it keeps Japan's security position closely aligned with the United States, but by suggesting a collective security arrangement, Ozawa and others have opened a very dangerous Pandora's box.

One other area of importance is the issue of trade in U.S.-Japan relations. This is going to be a difficult time for relations between these two countries because the Clinton administration is ready for action. Regardless of the personal relationship between Hosokawa and Clinton, a clear message has been sent from Washington: the $50 billion trade imbalance is unacceptable, and therefore, progress must be made to correct it. This time, as opposed to the 1980s, all of the figures in the administration are reading from the same page; there are no divisions in Washington. There is a very consistent, across-the-board position that this imbalance needs to be addressed. From Lloyd Bentsen to Ron Brown to Mickey Kantor, American policymakers want progress.

Discussions are being held about a framework, a fourfold division of how we can move forward. Automobiles and auto parts is the first area; additional progress should be made beyond the success of the Bush administration. (It was actually George Bush's biggest success in Tokyo. People only remember him sliding under the table after throwing up on the LDP's prime minister, but he did come out of that session with success on auto parts.) The framework set forth calls for movement in several other areas as well: telecommunications, medical equipment, and the insurance industry in Japan. The difficulty is how to measure movement in these areas. The agreement in Tokyo in July 1993 aimed at some measure of progress; however, whether that measure was to be quantitative or qualitative was unclear. The United States made it clear that they wanted quantitative measures. The bureaucrats in Japan backpedaled and said, "We don't want to manage trade. We have to figure out other ways to measure progress." Even though they failed to reach an agreement in February 1994, Bill Clinton was consistent in wanting Japan to show a measure of progress in the overall trade deficit.

Economists will often note that with the current exchange rate, deregulatory reform, and especially the tax cut and economic stimulus package, progress on the deficit ought to be measured by other numbers as well; however, it is not clear to me that Clinton is willing to wait for such long-term macroeconomic effects to come into play. The possibility of using sanctions allowed under the Super 301 trade provision is higher than it ever was before.

In short, Clinton has sent a strong message to the bureaucracy in Japan; moreover, he is right in letting not only the prime minister but also the bureaucracy know that the American position has hardened, not because Hosokawa has not made progress, but because Hosokawa is probably a lame duck prime minister. Specialists on Japan will often say, "Don't worry about the politicians; worry about the bureaucrats." Clinton's hardened position and bold moves probably conveyed most effectively his message to Japan's bureaucracy and thus motivated it to address the problem.

QUESTION: Do the terms *liberal democrats* and *socialists* have the same connotations in Japan as they do in the United States?

MR. ANDERSON: You have to be very cautious about how some English terms are translated into Japanese; what these terms mean in Japanese is not exactly the same as what they mean in English. The Liberal Democrats, for example, are liberal only in terms of their economic position. They have always been supporters of big business and a free-market economy. The Japan Socialists, on the other hand, have always wanted to plan Japan's economy more effectively, and their backers have always been Japan's larger unions.

It should be noted that both these camps have defined their identity along Cold War lines. The Liberal Democrats have based their position on Japan's alliance with the United States. The Socialists, on the other hand, have felt that such an alliance was not good for Japan. They took this position not because they wanted Japan to ally elsewhere as the Communists did, but because they advocated Japan's neutrality. They wanted to distance Japan from the United States and keep Japan from being drawn into any Cold War conflict.

With the Cold War over, both parties have had to undergo some redefinition of their party identity. The Socialists were savvy about this and changed their English name from the Japan Socialist Party to the Social Democratic Party as they saw their support slipping. I still call them the Socialists because they did not change their Japanese name and the Socialist Party is the best direct translation. Despite their attempt to redefine themselves and the party, however, they really failed to say what their new identity would be. As a result, the Japanese voter, as seen last July, does not know what to make of either party, and the Liberal Democrats were probably reelected on the basis of competence rather than a new redefinition of party identity. As people try to redefine and reposition themselves in the post-Cold War world and decide whether they are going to favor free-market principles or governmental involvement in the economy, I am not certain that either of these two parties will survive after the election reforms. (The socialists surprised me when the left wing abandoned their principles and formed a coalition with the Liberal Democrats. "Socialist" Prime Minister Tomiichi Murayama will have increasing trouble with his hold on power, however, under new election rules and a slow response to the Great Hanshin Earthquake in socialist-controlled Hyogo Prefecture.)

Perhaps even more critically, the Japanese are going to have to decide what Japan's post-Cold War role in international politics ought to be. Should Japan stay allied with the United States, or should Japan become an Asian power, defining their strategic interests as lying primarily in the Pacific Basin? Should Japan become a military political power that is independent of the United States?

QUESTION: Would it be fair to say that the Japanese economy is a managed free-enterprise economy? Second, what bearing do Japan's attitudes toward the rise in Asian competitiveness, a growing China, and their fears of that connection have on Japan's international outlook? Is Japan rethinking its identity as an Asian nation not in traditional terms, but in relation to the tremendous problems that lie ahead?

MR. ANDERSON: Regarding your reference to Japan being a managed free-trade or free-enterprise economy, I prefer to describe Japan as being a free market, *regulated* economy. I would remind you too that the United States economy, more than people like to admit, is also a regulated free-market economy. People ought to pay more attention to the meetings between Alan Greenspan of the Federal Reserve and Yasushi Mieno of the Bank of Japan. They should think about what principles in the U.S. economy keep its interest rates in line and about the Keynesian package of government spending. Americans should recognize the degree of regulation that exists in their own economy.

On the other hand, Japan really does have a much closer interaction between government and business. The Bank of Japan, for example, talks regularly to the equivalent of the U.S. Treasury at the Ministry of Finance and to the opposites of the National Association of Manufacturers at the Federation of Economic Organizations, Keidanren. Because there is much closer interaction between the public and private sectors in Japan, there is greater unity on government regulation.

By saying that the bureaucrats in Japan are very strong, I do not mean that everything is always pre-decided. Granted, there is a great deal of interaction and discussion, but one should recognize that the process of bringing all of the parties to the table and arriving at a decision is more effective in Japan than in many other countries.

Japan is not rethinking its relations with China in any radical way. Their response to the Tiananmen Square incident demonstrated Japan's unwillingness to confront the Chinese. Japan prefers to find ways of working with, not against, China. Even when world public opinion was against the Chinese government, Japan was reluctant to impose sanctions on its biggest foreign aid recipient. In fact, Japan never openly confronted the Chinese government, and rather than stop aid or impose sanctions, Japan merely delayed the dispersal of funds. Even when international outrage was greatest, Japan was still willing to meet regularly with China. Japan's foreign minister would meet with the Chinese leadership who wanted to meet as quickly as possible to avoid the condemnation of the international community. I think Japan sees its relations with China as key to its dealings with all of Asia. On the other hand, Japan also has strong relations with the Association of Southeast Asian Nations (ASEAN) and has been instrumental to the success of the Asia Pacific Economic Cooperation (APEC) meetings and conferences. In short, Japan appears to have a two-sided view of Asia, but neither one advocates confrontation with China. In that sense, many people in Japan still want to see "Asia for the Asians."

With respect to Japan's international outlook, there are primarily two groups in Japan. The first is the one just discussed. This group feels that Japan ought to focus on the Asia-Pacific. The other is comprised of those who are more internationalist and want to maintain strong economic relations with the United States and Europe. Those of the second group remain trilateralists in terms of their understanding of where Japan's economic stability is based. Nevertheless, the strength of the new Asian-oriented school should not be underestimated.

Speaking of Japan's economy reminds me of an article that appeared in today's *Washington Post* that suggests replacing the idea of Japan as the "Rising Sun" with "Rising Samd," which is a translation of the title of a Japanese magazine (for Uncle Sam, representing the return of U.S. competitiveness). With all due respect to T. R. Reed (the *Washington Post's* Japan correspondent), there are times when I think he is too "cute" in his comments. Though there are people looking at U.S. competitiveness in a new light, a reservoir of arrogance and dislike of feeling second class to the United States nevertheless remains in Asia, and I do not think that this emotion should be underestimated.

QUESTION: What is the Asian Pacific Economic Cooperation, usually referred to as APEC?

MR. ANDERSON: APEC is a process comprised of a series of meetings and conferences that were held in a broadly based effort to bring together the major countries of the Pacific Basin. In November 1993 the heads of state from the APEC nations,

127

including President Clinton and Prime Minister Hosokawa, gathered for the first time in Seattle, Washington, to support this effort. They formed a new secretariat to be based in Singapore, meaning that there will soon be an actual bureaucracy to better organize APEC's meetings. Some hope that APEC will become the basis for a type of European Community-style regional integration in the Pacific Basin, but it is a bit premature to make such a prediction. These countries are not as economically developed as the countries of Europe were in the early stages of the coal and steel arrangements that began the EC. Nevertheless, I do think that harmonization of some areas, like telecommunications standards or economic regulation, is fundamentally necessary to facilitate effective interaction among these dynamic economies. The APEC process could provide a key forum in which these countries could gather to talk about regulatory harmony among the various systems.

QUESTION: I have a minor question and a major one. First, what happens to Japan's used cars? Second, could you discuss the domestic politics of deregulation? I know a great deal about its form in the United States. A consumer movement and professional economists prescribed deregulation, but I cannot imagine what form it might take in Japan. Whence comes the impetus for domestic reform?

MR. ANDERSON: Regarding the used cars, my guess is that the Russians buy them (I'm half joking, of course). Shaken inspections doom many cars prematurely, which hurts consumers. On the issue of deregulation, it is very different in Japan. My quick answer to your question is that the impetus for domestic reform comes from above rather than below. In the 1980s, Margaret Thatcher in England and Ronald Reagan in America led deregulation. Meanwhile, in Japan there was Prime Minister Nakasone, but he was not talking about the horrors of government. He was talking about administrative reform, which meant specifically changing the degree of government control and management of the economy.

What Japan succeeded in doing was partly privatizing the national telephone system and splitting up the national railway system. Nevertheless, as I mentioned before, deregulation in Japan involves those at the top trying to split control of various industries by lessening the tools that the ministries have over private companies, by allowing products to be sold by smaller businesses, by breaking up very large economic and governmental agency regulations, and by introducing market principles. That is deregulation in Japan—not consumers saying they want more L. L. Bean-style catalogues—although the consumers are very happy to have benefited from these new initiatives and to have L. L. Bean and Toys "R" Us. These reforms have not taken place, however, because the consumer movement has been well organized.

The only way to really measure popular support in Japan is to look at the prime minister's popularity ratings with respect to certain key issues. The difference between the United States and Japan is that no one in Japan sees the efficacy of creating a small interest group that will then lobby the government and elect politicians. In the past that was never seen as a strong possibility. Perhaps after this new election reform system comes into effect, grass-roots movements will be more likely, particularly because a proportional representation (PR) system would encourage such interest groups to support candidates. Candidates in PR districts could be elected on the basis of single-issue politics. Whether they would have enough money to engage in the necessary campaign activities to attract votes and actually win in these new districts, however, remains to be seen. Nevertheless, Japan's experience with proportional representation in the less powerful Upper House shows that it is possible, as probably 10 percent of the candidates there were elected on the basis of single-issue problems like welfare.

In fact, welfare will be a huge problem for Japan. The demographics in Japan is likely to shift from the 12 percent of the population over the age of 65, as it was at the beginning of the decade, to 16 or 17 percent by the year 2000. Many people will want to ensure that they will receive the pensions to which they contributed and that they will have adequate medical care. Such issues could lead to the election of a special interest individual who would enter office with the particular mandate of maintaining welfare support. The same type of situation could evolve in the deregulation of the automobile industry. With time, the American model of deregulation might be more appropriate for Japan after all.

QUESTION: Why does the United States continue to press Japan on the dreadfully complex issue of rice? It is hardly a fight worth winning for people outside of Louisiana or Arkansas.

MR. ANDERSON: Anyone who thinks about trade has said the same thing and they always refer to a quote attributed to Ronald Reagan or his aides at Treasury. In the 1980s, when the United States fought Japan over trade issues, the Reagan man said, "Potato chips, computer chips, what difference does it make?" I think it makes a huge difference, and I agree with you entirely that rice is not a big-ticket item compared to automobiles, telecommunications equipment, computers, and software. These latter things are what could make the big difference in U.S.-Japan trade.

The reason rice is pursued as an issue is because of its symbolism. Rice is a symbolic issue in Japan because the Japanese have built up a whole cult of how rice made Japan different and how it is an intrinsic part of Japanese culture. The truth is that most of the commoners could not afford to eat rice for most of Japanese history; they had to eat barley instead. Only after World War II did rice become such a widespread and available commodity. Rice is also symbolic because of sake, which is rice wine, particularly given the emperor's involvement with the ritual process of making it.

Rice has become even more symbolic in terms of the international trading system, although Japanese bureaucrats had decided that this was the one issue on which they were not going to yield in terms of their position in the GATT. The Americans, however, felt that this was an easy issue on which to challenge Japan. They saw Japan as the country most benefiting from GATT and world trade and yet unwilling to import any rice whatsoever. Hence, rice became a very convenient symbol of Japan's unwillingness to meet the liberalization standards of the rest of the world. In short, the rice issue was not about money.

130

QUESTION: I am curious about the parliamentary districts. You said that completely new parliamentary districts were being established. Does gerrymandering take place in Japan? How will they set the boundaries?

MR. ANDERSON: For the first time in 70 years, gerrymandering will occur in Japan. No provision for gerrymandering existed previously. There was no real basis for using a census to change the districts. All they did was use the same lines, although sometimes they would pull a seat away from the countryside and give it to a suburban district to remedy the imbalance. Nevertheless, the imbalance was still close to six-to-one. A vote from the countryside was six times more powerful than one from a suburb of Tokyo. With the reforms, however, Japan is now going to have gerrymandering. I believe that when Hosokawa goes home from America, regardless of what he says here in the United States, he will be very busy addressing the concerns of the many politicians about where the lines are going to be drawn. Every weekend these politicians will be returning to their home districts to court the local interest groups, because political survival will be the only thing on their minds once the new districts are established. The word *Gerrymandering*, of which there is no equivalent in Japanese now, is going to become a Japanese word.

NARRATOR: We are grateful to Professor Anderson for this enlightening discussion. We are pleased that he is a part of the University of Virginia community and hope he will maintain that relationship for many years to come.[*]

---

[*] Anderson returned and reciprocates in this sentiment. Charlottesville and the Jeffersonian traditions will remain with his best memories of academic community. In fall 1994, Anderson did take a long-term research professorship at the Center for Global Communications of the International University of Japan, Dr. George Packard, president, where a new project will open access of the Internet into Japan [email = anderson@glocom.ac.jp]).

III

PATTERNS, PERSPECTIVES, AND PRINCIPLES

CHAPTER EIGHT

Human Rights in Historical and Cross-Cultured Perspectives*

SHAOZHONG PAN

NARRATOR: I would like to ask Professor Shao-chuan Leng to introduce our speaker. Professor Leng has been at the Miller Center for a number of years, and he is responsible for two very important volumes. *Coping With Crises: How Governments Deal with Emergencies* (1990) received notices as one of the best books of the year when it was published, and *Changes in China: Party, State, and Society* (1989) is an even more fundamental, significant contribution to the literature. A third volume is in preparation and will soon be available.

We have been proud of the fact that the Miller Center, under Professor Leng's leadership, has embarked on research on China and certain other Asian countries. Our Forum today, therefore, gives me the opportunity to pay tribute to him, a tribute that is well deserved and which he receives with very little pretense on his part.

MR. LENG: Thank you for your kind words. We are very privileged and honored to have as our speaker today, Professor Shaozhong Pan. Professor Pan was the dean of the Foreign Affairs College in Beijing, which trains Chinese foreign diplomats. He

---

Presented in a Forum at the Miller Center of Public Affairs on 18 June 1992.

remains a professor there in addition to serving as an associate of the Chinese Social Science Academy at the Institute of American Studies.

Professor Pan has been to the United States many times as a visiting professor at Yale University, the Woodrow Wilson Center in Washington, D.C., the East-West Center in Honolulu, and other institutions. He has also traveled widely and lectured on a variety of topics in Asia, the United States, and Europe. I could not begin to name the various institutions and topics he has covered, but he is an outstanding figure in the field of American studies in China.

MR. PAN: Thank you very much. I hope that I can live up to the kind words of Professor Leng. I am going to speak this morning on human rights. As you probably know from Professor Leng's introduction, I am neither a political scientist nor a jurist; yet, the topic of human rights is generally handled from either a political science or an international law angle. I specialize, however, in comparative culture—especially comparison of American and Chinese culture—and I propose to discuss this topic with you today from what I call a historical, cross-cultural perspective. I will also try to discuss the current human rights situation in China.

Whenever people talk about human rights, there usually is some confusion in terminology. What is meant by human rights? People argue about this all over the world because of the various interpretations of the concept. For instance, some people regard human rights as individual rights, while others regard them as collective rights. Still others view human rights in a purely economic or political sense.

I will not get into that kind of an academic debate today. One very important thing to remember about the concept of human rights as individual rights, however, is what John Dewey said long ago about the individuality of culture. As Dewey put it in his work *Freedom & Culture*, which was published in 1939:

> The function of culture in determining what elements of human nature are dominant and their pattern or arrangement in connection with one another goes beyond any special point to which attention is called. It affects the very idea of individuality;

the idea that human nature is inherently and exclusively individual is itself a product of a cultural, individualistic movement. The idea that the mind and consciousness are intrinsically individual did not even occur to anyone for much of the greater part of human history.

I take this statement as my text, because it sets the whole problem or question in its historical and cultural perspective. For if one talks about human rights as rights of human beings *per se*, they are a kind of individual rights that might be economic, social, or political. In this sense, human rights are a modern concept, and in particular, a Western concept. Looking at several major religions, one sees why John Dewey mentioned individuality as having been in the mind of human beings for only a short period of time. In Islam, Hinduism, and Buddhism, there was no such tradition.

What about the Judeo-Christian traditions from which all Western civilizations developed? Without going into detail, the fact is that even in the Judeo-Christian traditions the idea of human rights as individual rights began very late. I would suggest that the idea began during the Renaissance and developed during the Reformation, the Enlightenment, and the American and French Revolutions. Through these historical movements that originated in the West, the idea of human rights began to be accepted by more and more people. It was not, however, accepted to any significant extent until the Second World War, when the Holocaust brought most of mankind to a realization that it is essential to have basic human rights and some sort of general and universally accepted criteria concerning those rights.

If you look at American history, you will find that at first, human rights were not generally accepted. Religious tolerance actually came to the states much later than it did to England. Even after the Constitution of the United States and the Bill of Rights were passed, the status of human rights still left much to be desired in the states. Only through a long historical and cultural process, did human rights come to be known as they are in the United States today.

When traditional Chinese culture traits and the evolution of the concept of human rights in China are examined, we find that a number of major differences distinguish traditional Chinese culture from American or Western European culture. These differences grew after Western Europe entered the Renaissance period and then with each of the subsequent great movements that I mentioned.

Although there is much in traditional Chinese culture conducive to the evolution of human rights, the Chinese have not had the same understanding of human rights that Americans have today. For instance, in traditional Chinese culture, there is a pronounced element of secularism. We Chinese have generally not had a state religion; instead, throughout most of our history, we had a state philosophy: Confucianism. Among the common people, this philosophy consisted basically of a kind of ancestor worship plus some elements of Buddhism, but it was very much secularized and constituted the prevailing criteria of ethics in China.

One of the basic tenets of Confucianism is that one should be a secular person working for the group. In this principle lie the basics of individualism, but with a big difference. Confucianism regards the secular individual only as a member of a certain group. I will say something more about this later, but again, this kind of secularism is important to Chinese history and to the understanding of Chinese culture.

Throughout most of Confucian teachings and writings, you will find that the people as a whole have always been regarded as the basis of the country or, to use a figure of speech from Chinese culture, "as the water that could either float the boat of government or sink it." This idea was obviously very important, but it does not reflect the same idea as does the Western concept of democracy. The Confucian tradition simply meant that the rulers or the government would have to prove their Mandate of Heaven through the support of the people. They, therefore, would have to cherish the people and pay attention to the people so that the people would support them and their mandate.

The Chinese have also imbibed many Buddhist teachings, one of which is the Buddhist concept of mercy. Buddha taught that the world was one of misery, so one had to be good to others and show mercy to others in order to alleviate the suffering of this world and prepare oneself for the next world, which was of the highest importance. I am sure that this idea is common to most religions, but it shows that even the Buddhist concept of mercy does not comprise the idea of individuality.

The Confucian and Buddhist teachings were once thought by Western scholars to be in line with concepts of individualism, democracy, and similar concepts, especially in the 18th century, when these academics served to promote the great movement of the Enlightenment. These ideas, however, were not properly understood in their Chinese context. It was only later that the Europeans began to see the teachings of Confucianism as rather hierarchical and autocratic.

Other constraints in Chinese culture also run counter to the Western tradition of individuality. The first is group orientation. Confucian teaching centered around the idea that the individual should work for the benefit of the group and that the group should come first. In China, we say that you have to cultivate your mind. Although such a maxim appears individualistic, the Chinese believe you should cultivate your mind so that you can maintain peace in your family, promote your community, and help run the country. Literally, the Chinese believed that one's purpose was "to try to bring about peace under heaven," so the basic responsibilities of the scholar who cultivated his mind were toward the group, beginning with the family and ending with the country. At one time, most Chinese regarded China as the center of the world, so their responsibility ended there.

Chinese culture has also traditionally been dominated by ethics. Ethics came first among most of the Confucian teachings. You had to cultivate your mind because you had to foster a strong sense of responsibility, and all of your actions were to be guided by Confucian teachings. The dominating role of ethics helped the Chinese hierarchies and dynasties to maintain their rule over the people. It did not involve much individualism.

In modern Chinese history, which generally is viewed as the period since the first Opium War in 1839, the number-one question for most Chinese—at least for the elite—has been that of national salvation. China's subjection to foreign invasion and the danger of national subjugation led to concern over how to save China as a nation, a country, and a culture. When that goal was realized, the primary question became, In a modified manner, how could China catch up with the West and how could it modernize? Historically, therefore, the group has always been the central concern in China.

That brings us to the period following the Communist Party's takeover in 1949. If human rights are perceived as collective and economic rights being considered first and foremost, it could be said that there has been much improvement in human rights since 1949. In the area of women's rights, for example, this improvement is very obvious. Before 1949, polygamy was more or less legal in China. I say more or less because, although there was a law mandating monogamy, it was not enforced. In practice, therefore, there was actual polygamy. The women were taught to abide by the so-called three obediences and four virtues. In practice, this meant she was to obey her father before marriage. After marriage, she was to obey her husband, and if her husband died, she was to obey her son. Legally, women simply had no rights. In actuality, of course, some women did wield power. That situation has been abolished in most cases, although there are exceptions—especially in the rural areas.

A typical case of improved economic rights concerns life expectancy and the so-called human development index. In an attempt to evaluate the progress of a country in human terms, it does not make much sense to say that people are free to say whatever they want when at the same time they are dying of starvation. It makes the least sense of all to the Chinese, who have always believed that food is the heaven of the people. Without that, they believe no rights are possible.

The United Nations Development Program (UNDP) and its human development index show this attitude to be true in practice. The overarching index is composed of a number of more general indexes, but they mainly concern three components: life expectancy, education, and income. With those three things, life is more or less guaranteed. In classifying the 160 countries in the world according to those criteria, the United Nations places China as number 59— rather above the average. In terms of per capita GNP, however, China is placed 110th—much below the average. Such a significant difference reflects clearly that China has made much progress in the area of using social wealth for the benefit of the general population.

140

That explanation may be somewhat incomplete, but we can discuss it further during the question period.

Finally, let us discuss the human rights situation in the post-Mao period. What progress has been demonstrated during this period? There are at least three or four fields to which one should pay attention. The most important change of this period is in the concept of human rights.

According to orthodox Marxist ideology, human rights, as now defined, do not exist in a class society, which means practically all societies on earth at present. There are only class rights in a class society in which all human beings are divided economically and politically into classes. Thus, Communists traditionally have always opposed the idea of human rights. For the first 30 years of their rule, the Chinese Communists were no exception.

After the Cultural Revolution, however, they came to realize two things. First, through their own experiences, the leaders—including Deng Xiaoping—began to realize that there needed to be some guarantee of human rights, even for those such as Deng Xiaoping, who was high up in the Communist hierarchy. Otherwise, anyone could suffer the kind of indignities and inhumanities that the leaders themselves experienced during the Cultural Revolution. Secondly, the Communist leadership realized that much progress in human rights had been made in the world, and China could no longer be satisfied with her own achievements in terms of economic and collective rights. Beginning in the mid-1970s, as a consequence of these realizations, China began to acknowledge that such a thing as human rights did exist, and this was a great breakthrough. As a result, China signed six or seven pacts on human rights. This recognition is significant, because it suggests that there is now a basis for discussing and improving human rights in China, which was duly recorded in its 1982 Constitution.

In reflecting upon the entire post-Mao period, there has been material progress in this area, and many of the so-called wrong verdicts—the persecutions of the past—were remedied partly or substantially. There is a stronger rule of law as well. Still, problems remain, and unfortunately, some of these improvements were interrupted and thrown back by the notorious Tiananmen Square incident of 1989.

China remains constrained by a number of elements. First are the so-called four cardinal principles. China is still committed to the Communist Party and socialism as its state ideology. Regardless of how pragmatic and liberal the Communists try to seem, communism remains a constraint and will continue to do so for the foreseeable future.

The second and most important constraining element is the Chinese drive for stability and economic prosperity. Before the Tiananmen Square incident, some people believed that China had not experienced any political reform and that the Chinese should learn from the changes in the Soviet Union. After what happened in Eastern Europe and Russia, however, some people, including many intellectuals, had a change of heart. For instance, when I was in China during the Tiananmen incident in June 1989, a number of people, especially among intellectuals, were hoping that Deng Xiaoping would die as soon as possible so that Zhao Ziyang could take over, and things would begin to change. Today, however, the dominant hope is that Deng Xiaoping will live long enough to confirm China's opening to the outside world. People are beginning to pray for a longer life for Deng Xiaoping, because they view long-term stability and economic progress as essential to China.

Another aspect of Chinese culture relevant to the issue of human rights is that the Chinese still tend to see the country and the family, not the individual, as society's basic units. China's attitude toward abortion and family planning is a case in point. This is a very emotional and controversial question in the United States. In this country, the debate is between those who call themselves pro-life and those who call themselves pro-choice. The pro-life position, apart from its religious basis, essentially suggests that a life from its very beginning has rights. The human rights argument for the pro-life position is that the embryo has human rights. The pro-choice view is very different, but it is also a human rights argument, with the concern being for what these individuals consider to be the woman's individual right to choose whether or not to have a baby.

Explaining how this question is viewed in China might give you some insight into the Chinese mind. In China, there are also two camps, but theoretically, everyone is unified on one question: What

142

will constitute China's biggest problem for the next century or so? It is not which party is going to lead China, or which nationality is going to dominate, but what is to be done about China's population problem. China's current population is almost 1.2 billion—almost one quarter of the world's population—and even though the growth rate is much better than it is in most developing countries, it is still a very explosive situation. By the end of this century, China's population will probably be 1.3 billion, and if there is no vigorous family planning, the population will reach 1.5 billion by the year 2020.

China has more than four times the population of the United States but only one-third the arable land. Because there is also little room for land reclamation in China, most scientists there have agreed that, with her own resources, China can, at most, feed 1.5 billion people living a modestly comfortable life. If its population were to increase beyond that number, it would create a dangerous situation for both China and the rest of the world. Consequently, the Chinese people are generally in agreement that they must control the population, and as a result, each couple should only have one, or at most two, children.

Beyond that general consensus, however, there are quite a few Chinese, especially in the rural areas, who want more children for the benefit of their own families. If the family does not have a male child, they fear being without linear offspring and ending the family line. These people are still thinking of a group—the family—albeit a much smaller one.

I submit, therefore, that the Chinese people still regard human rights basically as a matter of economic and group rights, including the right to survival, the right to a better life, and the right to work. These are rights that can usually be measured by the human development index and by life expectancy, and both are areas in which China has improved greatly over the last half century. Life expectancy in China in 1949 was a mere 35 years, worse than life expectancy in India. Today it is about 70 years. This increase has been achieved through a number of factors, but I venture to suggest that it probably also shows material progress in the area of human rights, despite the negative impact of the Tiananmen Square incident.

QUESTION: You mentioned that if China's population exceeds 1.5 billion, it may create a danger for China and for the world as well. Could you be more specific as to what form that danger will take in the world?

MR. PAN: That is a good question because it is difficult to envisage that sort of danger. Let me give you two concrete examples to illustrate the type of problems that might result. One example concerns Bangladesh. Bangladesh has an area smaller than that of California, but it has a population almost one-half as large as that of the United States—over 100 million. It is an impossible situation that no party or politician could solve. The situation has resulted in massive suffering at home and a huge refugee problem for the country's neighbors. As poor as India is, India receives many economic refugees from Bangladesh. There is, of course, also the question of how to feed the people of Bangladesh, who usually have only one meal per day and have to eke out their existence from that.

My second example involves emigration. When Deng Xiaoping visited the United States for the first time in 1978, it is said that Jimmy Carter asked whether the Chinese government would relax its policies on emigration, given legal restrictions on U.S. trade relations with Communist countries. Deng Xiaoping asked Carter point-blank how many Chinese immigrants he wanted in the United States every year, 5 million or 50 million. Carter reportedly did not respond to that, and emigration was never again regarded as a problem between China and the United States until the Tiananmen Square incident in 1989. Those are two illustrations of the kind of problems China and the world might face given an unstable China with little economic growth and a population out of control.

QUESTION: Until the late 1970s, observers of East Asia identified the East Asian Confucian heritage as an impediment to modern economic achievement. Since then, however, many of the same observers and others identify that heritage as a significant stimulant to economic development. Do you think such a change in attitude and interpretation might occur in the future with regard to human rights and, in particular, individual rights in China?

144

Shaozhong Pan

There are examples in Chinese history of a tendency toward individuality, if not full-scale individualism, generated from within Confucianism. I am referring specifically to developments in the late 16th century that did not last, but nonetheless provide an example of a Confucian-stimulated interest in individuality. The historical situation at that time may not have been right, but I wonder whether there will be a time when a Chinese conception of individual rights might develop from within the Confucian heritage.

MR. PAN: This question concerns a topic that I am particularly partial to, which is how the Confucian heritage is viewed. The Confucian heritage is very complex, and I do not think any Confucian scholar today can claim that he has exhausted all of its possibilities. There appears to be many impediments to modern progress in Confucianism. For example, the so-called three obediences and four virtues of Chinese women were shaped basically by Confucian scholars, and they are obviously an impediment to development.

Confucian ideology has also traditionally focused on the peasants as the foundation of society, while the elite, scholars, bureaucrats, and other members of the highest echelons were viewed as the rulers of the country. The merchants, the handicraftsmen, and the burghers, who actually gave rise to modern capitalism, were despised, and efforts were made to eliminate their influence, which was also a great impediment to progress in China. A third important obstacle to modernization resulted from Confucian disdain for profit. Chinese scholars and bureaucrats always emphasized ruling the country with the ideas of benevolent government and interhuman relations. Practical learning was not regarded as important or high-class, but instead as the least of the learnings.

As illustrated, the ideology of Confucianism as created by scholars of the past posed barriers to China's progress. China was one of the world's most advanced countries in the 3rd century B.C. and maintained that position, not only economically and militarily, but also technologically and scientifically, for almost 18 centuries—until around the 16th century. When the industrial revolution occurred in Western Europe, however, China began to lag further and further behind. Confucianism, *per se*, probably was suited to

145

the earlier periods and the Asian culture but was not conducive to modernization as it is understood today.

Still, the subject is complex because there are also quite a few elements in Confucianism that are useful and might be adapted to modern times, as is obvious in East Asia today. It is important to understand, however, that there are two sides of Confucianism. One, which most people in China today still espouse, taught that stability was of the utmost importance and that an authoritarian government was conducive to stability. Therefore, most new industrial countries began with that kind of system, and after a while, its disadvantages became more and more serious.

Another side of the Confucian heritage, however, might be helpful to modernization. Confucian teachings have always stressed education, diligence, and hard work. That can be seen not only in East Asia, but also in the United States and wherever else there is an East Asian, particularly Chinese, population. Still this does not mean that Confucian ideology per se is conducive to modernization.

Regarding prospects for human rights in China, I believe that you must be very patient with the Chinese. After all, China has a written history of 3,000 years. In China, history is not counted in years or decades, but in centuries. If you view the situation from that perspective, the prospects for human rights, even in terms of individual rights, are bright in China.

Look at Taiwan, which is part of China, and at what has happened there over the last 40 years. For most of that period, Taiwan was a military and police state under rigorous governmental control. Since then, however, a flourishing economy, a stronger middle class, and an opening to the outside world has made it impossible to hold back the current of human rights. Taiwan has begun to liberalize more and more, and there will be no turning back the tide.

With Deng Xiaoping's consistent line of reform and opening to the outside world, China will experience stability and economic progress for the next 10 or 20 years, and the inevitable result will be greater respect for human rights in China. I am very confident of that over the long term. Reform, however, must come from within, not from without.

146

Pressure from the outside, especially crude pressure that would hurt the self-respect of the Chinese, will not help. The international community can only help by encouraging the reforms and the opening up of China to the outside world. Eventually, this will lead to increased respect for human rights, a better life for the Chinese people, and therefore, better prospects for the world. Whatever compromises or arrangements are needed, the Chinese will work out themselves. In the final analysis, human rights in China is their affair, not the affair of anyone else.

QUESTION: How will China treat Hong Kong when the two merge in the future?

MR. PAN: First, the importance of Hong Kong to China must be understood. China receives 70 percent of her total foreign exchange income and 80 percent of her foreign investment through Hong Kong—which includes Taiwan, because Taiwan currently does everything through Hong Kong. In terms of individual private foreign investment, more than 20 billion U.S. dollar have been invested in China. No Chinese leader is so foolish as to try to kill a goose that lays golden eggs.

Second, China is now inseparably linked to Hong Kong. In fact, the market-oriented Southern coastal region of China, including Guangdong province, resembles Hong Kong but is even bigger. Hong Kong has five to six million people, but Guangdong province—where the people speak the same dialect as in Hong Kong—there are 63 million people. In manufacturing, Hong Kong employs only 700,000 workers in her current territory, but employs two million workers in Guangdong. If China were to, consciously or unconsciously, destabilize Hong Kong, it would mean catastrophe for China as well. When all is said and done, one has to bear in mind that stability is the primary prerequisite for China. Therefore, China will not tolerate anything that appears to destabilize Hong Kong.

NARRATOR: In discussing human rights, there has always been contention between those who say that human rights are fundamentally political rights and therefore, social and economic matters

147

should be handled through legislation—not through declarations or covenants—and those who say that political, social, and economic rights are inseparable from each other. The history of U.S. relations with the Soviet Union shows how disruptive the differences can be in terms of international relations. Is there any way that you can see people from these two perspectives coming to understand one another in the years ahead?

MR. PAN: With due respect for Professor Leng and other political scientists here, I would say that political scientists will go on arguing about those differences forever. Scholars of culture see the issue more simply because they believe in cultural pluralism, which essentially means that people think differently and act differently. In China, there is a saying: "The well-fed man doesn't know the troubles of the hungry man." In other words, for those who are well fed, political rights will probably come first, because they are not faced with the problem of starvation. The United States, for example, has only faced the problem of starvation during several brief periods. The first settlers were threatened with starvation, and during the Civil War, some Southerners faced it. There was also a rather long period of time during the Great Depression when the poor did not have enough to eat. Apart from those short periods, however, Americans have never known actual deprivation.

For the Chinese, the question of survival has always been the number-one concern. American journalist Theodore White reported that in 1940, five million people died of sheer starvation during a great famine in the Henan Province caused by bad drought and corrupt government. Starvation is not a rare experience in China. During the Communist reign, with Mao's utopian ideas and bad management, many died of slow or acute starvation—20 million in just a three-to-four-year period, according to some people.

To come back to your question, I believe the question of human rights within the context of the specific circumstances of each and every country would need to be discussed. What is most important is not declarations, pacts, or legislation, but actual practice. I did not cite the articles of the Chinese Constitution in my talk because they do not mean much. What people actually have and get is what is most important.

For the next 10 or 20 years, the Chinese people will continue to be primarily interested in their economic and social rights, in having enough food and a better life. As these requirements are satisfied, however, the Chinese people will find that this is not enough, and they will struggle for more and more rights. That is why I say that in the next century, there will be big changes in China in terms of human rights. I am fervently praying for that.

NARRATOR: We appreciate this well-informed and wide-ranging discussion of a problem that we read about but which takes on much greater meaning when we hear about it firsthand. Thank you very much, Professor Pan.

CHAPTER NINE

China's Model of Development: Insights from China's Reform Experiences of 15 Years*

CAIBO WANG

NARRATOR: I first met Caibo Wang at China's Jilin University during a trip for the United States Information Agency (USIA). I discovered then that we had a mutual interest in political culture. I also discovered that in addition to teaching courses in American government and comparative government at Jilin University, she is also a specialist in the field of American political thought and Western political thought.

Dr. Wang first came to the United States as a visiting scholar at Rutgers University. Now, on her second visit, she is a senior Fulbright scholar conducting research at the University of California at Berkeley. Thanks to the Fulbright grants, she is able to visit the Miller Center.

Professor Wang is only the second person to graduate in political science at Jilin University and only one of two political scientists teaching at the university—the discipline of political science as we know it did not exist in China until after the Cultural Revolution—where she is an associate professor and the head of the political theory division. Among her many accomplishments is a

---

Presented in a Forum at the Miller Center of Public Affairs on 20 April 1994, James S. Young, narrator.

translation of Robert Nozick's *Anarchy, State, and Utopia* into Chinese. Her own publications have included works on American theories of political socialization, principles of political science, the teaching of political science, the British political system, and Canadian political issues, particularly relations between English- and French-speaking Canadians. It is a great pleasure to welcome her.

MS. WANG: The rapid economic development in China, which began a few years after the Cultural Revolution (1966-1976), has drawn increasingly more attention from the outside world. How does one explain the great changes that have been occurring in China and how does one predict the future? These issues grew more important and interesting over time. As a scholar from China, I have the responsibility of presenting an analysis of China's reform and the nature of its rapid changes in relation to the outside world.

I would like to begin by presenting the facts about China's economic reform and development. China's economic reform policies have brought about the rapid development of its economy, and consequently profound changes in the social value system, the structure of society, and politics. As an important part of my discussion, I will provide some analysis of China's model of political development. My point of view is that China's political development will take place through economic development; that is, China's economic development will promote political change and political development. This model has, in fact, been adopted by the Chinese government for a number of reasons, three aspects in particular that have been most compelling: (1) China's historical and current reality, (2) lessons from the former U.S.S.R.'s reform experiences, and (3) the development experiences of other Eastern Asian countries.

I. China's Economic Reform and Economic Development

China's economic reform policy has primarily involved the opening up of the nation to the outside world. Despite the ups and downs in the process of economic reform of the past 15 years,

Caibo Wang

China has taken five important steps that are representative of its overall adherence to the reform path. First, China's economic reform began with the decollectivization of rural agriculture. Before the reform, agricultural production in China took place on collectivist people's communes that were designed with a centralized structure of unified distribution and management, the work-point system based on collective labor, and the centralized purchasing and marketing of agricultural products. Under this collectivist system, agricultural productivity was relatively low.

The first and most significant step of agricultural reform was the decentralization of this structure. At the end of 1978, reform policy established a household contract system, which decollectivized agriculture by making rural households the predominant force in the newly self-managed rural economy. By December 1984, 99 percent of the country's production brigades—the basic units under the collectivist people's commune system—had adopted the new system. Under the household contract system, the village committee, formerly known as the production brigade, contracts land out to families for farming and collects a tax on the land, which is then used to finance collective undertakings such as irrigation. Peasants are free to market their surpluses, to develop sidelines, and to engage in a range of economic activities previously forbidden.

These measures have greatly liberalized productivity in agriculture. Under the household contract system, China's 800 million peasants have been freed from the state-controlled economy, thereby unleashing the initiative, energy, and drive so lacking in the previous system. As a consequence, productivity has grown rapidly and the living standards of peasant-farmers have improved significantly.

The second step of the reform process has been the encouragement and rise of small entrepreneurs in rural and urban areas. Under this policy, private, collective, and joint-venture entrepreneurship is now allowed in China. In the rural areas, this growth has been clearly evident in the development of township enterprises, which have been important for Chinese economic development. During the 13 years from 1978 to 1991, the number of township enterprises increased from 1.52 million to 19.08 million, and total employment increased by 70 million. Total income of township

153

enterprises increased from 43.2 billion in 1978 to 1,500 billion yuan in 1992, while total profits and taxes increased from 11 billion yuan to 150 billion yuan during the same period. In the cities, urban private and joint-venture enterprises have substantially increased. By 1992, private, collective, and foreign joint-venture enterprises had produced more than half of the national income.

The third step is best characterized by the decentralization of economic control, through fiscal decentralization, which has increased the fiscal power of provincial and local governments, enabling them to stimulate the economy on their own initiative. Provincial and local governments now have considerable latitude to raise their own funds and take whatever action is necessary to develop their respective region's economies. This freedom has unleashed the powerful competitive dynamism of the provinces, since an economically successful region can gain more benefits than an unsuccessful region. As a result, regional competition for foreign funds and for the fruits of economic success has been another key factor in China's development. Within China, provinces compete with provinces. Within provinces, cities compete with cities, towns compete with towns, and similarly down to the lowest levels of social organization. This competitive energy has generated the internal dynamic of economic development within China, and has encouraged the development of local infrastructure across the nation.

The fourth step has been the establishment of special economic zones (SEZ), which have been given special authority to attract foreign investment. Under this policy, foreign enterprises and joint-ventures grow rapidly in the special economic zones, which attracts a considerable amount of foreign funds. The creation of special economic zones began in 1979 in the coastal areas. These zones were designed to attract foreign capital, expertise, and technology to help develop domestic Chinese export industries. Financial incentives were provided for foreign investors, but occupants were not permitted to sell their products in the mainland market. The rules have, however, been relaxed somewhat over the years.

Slow to start in the early days, foreign investment in these zones has increased tremendously over the past seven to eight years, with funds coming mainly from overseas Chinese sources, especially from Hong Kong. More recently, investment sources from Taiwan, Singapore, Malaysia, and Indonesia have increased significantly, and investors from South Korea, Japan, Europe, and North America have also found an interest in China. As the success of SEZs has become more widely recognized and as central control of the economy has eased, many other provinces and local governments have begun forming their own special development areas. These regional and local SEZs attract an astonishing amount of foreign investment.

The fifth step in this process was the adoption of a dual-price system and a dual foreign-currency exchange system. Unlike the sudden price liberalization that occurred in the former Soviet Union and Eastern European countries, China has liberalized prices in a gradual and careful way. First, it adopted a dual-price system; that is, it allowed the prices of some goods be determined by the market, while others remained state-fixed. The idea was to ensure that the price of rice and other daily necessities would not become so volatile as to threaten the living standards of ordinary people. By 1992, as a result of this gradual price liberalization program, the majority of prices were determined by the market, including over 70 percent of consumer goods and industrial materials. Even many agricultural and industrial input prices were deregulated by 1992. In September 1992 the government made deeper reforms, freeing the prices of all goods except 111 production materials (down from 737) and delegated control of 22 other production materials to the direct authority of the localities. An important aspect of China's price reform policy has been to gradually adjust state-controlled prices upward until they eventually reach market levels. Although price reform still has a long way to go, China has shown that such reform can be achieved without the same catastrophes that occurred in Eastern Europe. China's dual-price foreign-currency exchange system has been unified since January 1994—a transition that has also gone smoothly.

China's economic reform has resulted in tremendous achievements, namely, the rapid growth of the economy. From 1978 to 1993, China's average GNP growth was 9 percent, making it the fastest growing economy in the world. In 1992 the overall GNP growth rate reached 12.8 percent, and in 1993 the GNP growth rate was 13.4 percent. Foreign trade has also grown tremendously, and in 1992 China became the tenth largest exporter of goods in the world. Between 1978 and 1992, China's total trade volume rose by over 800 percent, from U.S. $20.66 billion to U.S. $165.6 billion, ranking China's trade volume eleventh in the world. In 1992 alone, China's direct foreign investment reached $11.2 billion. In 1978 China had signed 36 contracts with two countries, valued at $51 million. By 1991 the number had grown to 8,438 contracts worth over $36 billion with 147 countries and regions.

As a result, the population's living standard has greatly improved and average incomes have doubled. The World Bank reported in a 1993 study that the proportion of Chinese living in absolute poverty—lacking decent food, housing, and clothing—dropped from 220 million in 1980 to 100 million in 1990. This means that while there were still 100 million people in China living in absolute poverty in 1990, the overall number had nevertheless been cut in half.

There are now sufficient supplies in urban and rural markets in China. Private, collective, and state-owned stores are full of different kinds of goods. The foreigners visiting China recently have all been impressed by the dazzling Chinese markets. Chinese people have, in fact, never before lived better. China's countryside experienced its largest income increase of 14.5 percent between 1978 to 1984. From 1978 to 1982, income in rural areas as well as in urban areas grew by 6.9 percent.

II. The Impact of Economic Reform and Development on Chinese Society

China's economic reform and development have had a profound impact on other areas of the society. First, many ideas and ways of thinking have undergone a profound change during the course of reform. Before 1979 China was a very closed society. Except for a little knowledge about the former U.S.S.R. and other socialist countries, ordinary Chinese people knew little about the outside world and had no idea about the Western world at all.

Under the opening up policy, Chinese people for the first time since 1949 had opportunities for exposure to the outside world, especially the Western world. Communication with the outside world has made the Chinese people realize how far China has fallen behind in respect to economic, scientific, and technical development as a result of the disastrous ten-year Cultural Revolution. People realized what a low standard of living China had compared to those of advanced countries. Before the reforms, the Chinese made only vertical comparisons to gauge development; that is, an analysis through China's history, emphasizing how much progress China has made since 1949. As a result, even though the country was comparatively backward, there was an unrealistically optimistic view of the country's circumstances. Only recently have the Chinese begun to make horizontal comparisons between China's development and that of other countries.

I have personal knowledge of this type of thinking. When I attended middle school, the teachers taught us that the Chinese were the happiest people in the world. We did not know anything of the outside world, so we believed what we had been taught. Now that communication has put the Chinese in contact with the outside world, Chinese people as well as policymakers recognize China's backwardness.

The country's economic reform policy of putting economic development first has gained a wide-ranging consensus from society. During the initial process of economic reform, the overall living standard of the Chinese people increased significantly. Having experienced the fruits of economic reform and development, political approval and support of economic reform is getting stronger and stronger. The development of a market economy has generated opportunities and choices that have never before been experienced in the history of new China.

The emergence of the market economy has spurred competition and increased incentive for profit. Seeing that they can actually improve their living standard and physical circumstances through hard work and initiative, people have welcomed the process of economic reform. Since there were no economic differences between the circumstances of those who worked hard and those who did not under the planned economy, people had no initiative and

157

therefore did not work hard. With the reforms and an increasingly open economy, people now see that there is something to be gained from hard work. These changes have redirected the focus of most people to economic matters. The market economy has encouraged the rise of an entrepreneurial spirit that was missing in the old economic system and in all areas of China.

The process of economic reform and development has also resulted in some fundamental changes in China's social structure. The emergence of diversified interests has provided the basis for these changes. Before reform, China had a unitary and rigid social structure based on a relatively fixed social status system in which upward movement was determined by factors such as power and position. It was not directly linked to the factors of income and education, which have been the basic determining elements of social status in Western societies. Under China's previous social structure, people pursued status by pursuing power through position promotion. While income was only a by-product of status promotion, it could not determine social status in the society.

During the period of economic reform, China's resource allocation underwent a great deal of change. Accompanying changes in resource transfers were the corresponding changes in social structure. In the new economic system, resources are transferred mostly to the people with lower power and lower position. Changes in resource allocation have shifted the once tight relationship between position, power, and income to a relatively looser relationship between these factors. Income has become a relatively independent factor in judging the status of people, as power and position are no longer the sole determinants. Now people can achieve a higher social status by increasing their income levels.

The changes in the transfer of resources have demonstrated the rational existence of independent economic interests. Before the reforms, people were taught to pursue common interests. If a person pursued individual interests, he or she was certain to be criticized because such interests were not considered to be good. Recent changes, however, now encourage the independent pursuit of economic interests. Through the process of resource transfers and the diversification of interests, new social classes and strata have formed—strata that never existed in the previous system—such as business owners, self-employed people, entrepreneurs, and staff members in foreign, joint-venture, and private enterprises.

Economic reform has not only brought the formation of new social classes and strata, but also the fundamental transformation of the old social classes. For example, tremendous changes have taken place in the rural structure. Although 70 to 80 percent of China's population still live in the rural areas, employment in agriculture has decreased by 26 percent, from 69 percent in 1980 to 43 percent in 1991. The proportion of rural enterprises, however, increased by 22 percent over the same period. In other words, while a high percentage of China's population still lives in rural areas, many rural people are no longer traditional peasants. This is a profound change because these two fundamental shifts in the social structure suggest that China's reform trajectory is permanent and irreversible.

The third transformation has occurred in the political arena, where the impact of economic reform and development have also resulted in some remarkable changes. In China, ideology is being superseded by the everyday convergence of factors necessary to be politically, economically, and socially competitive. In recent years, China has consciously de-emphasized ideology and ideological fervor for a much more pragmatic philosophy. Economic pragmatism has become the driving force behind much of the central government's policy. Gone are the endless discussions about what socialism should be and the distinctions between socialism and capitalism. In their place are discussions to determine what will facilitate China's development, how to increase people's living standards, and how to modernize the country. The implementation of China's reform program has been based on this pragmatic philosophy, and its tremendous success has further propelled and enhanced practical thinking. Recent reform experiences and the lessons of history have made both the ordinary people and the policymakers abandon unrealistic dogma and adopt a more pragmatic way of thinking. This fundamental change in thinking and philosophy demonstrates considerable progress.

The country's political atmosphere is totally different from the atmosphere before the reform period, especially that of the Cultural Revolution. It is even fundamentally different from what it was four or five years ago. Every foreigner who has been in China recently can discern the difference. People are now more likely to speak their minds, and the range of discussion has widened. Economic reform has reduced the Communist Party's role in people's private lives. In fact, historically the Chinese people have never been more free than they are now.

The waning role of the *danwei*, or work unit, has also added to the growing sense of individual freedom. In the past, all people were attached to a work unit that determined not only promotions, salaries, and housing, but also other matters such as whether they could get married or travel. The unit kept each worker's dossier, which listed biographical as well as political information. In contrast, an increasing number of people now work outside the work-unit system, going into business for themselves, or working for foreign companies. As an entrepreneur, an individual must rely on himself or herself to make a living and is free from the control of the *danwei*. Even those who belong to work units enjoy increasing degrees of freedom, however. Currently, most Chinese opt to live within the society's present system and concentrate on getting ahead. One should bear in mind that many of the best and brightest of China's new generation are seeking freedom as well as their fortunes in China's booming market economy.

III. The Model of China's Political Development

One of the most important characteristics of China's model of development is that economic reform has occurred in the context of a relatively stable and unchanged socio-political structure. Why did China have to assume this model of development? First, the model suits China's real situation, which is unique in some aspects. In China, 20 percent of the earth's population now lives on 7 percent of the earth's land and only 14 percent of this land is arable. About 70 to 80 percent of the people continue to live in the countryside. In addition, nearly 20 percent of the population continues to be illiterate, most of whom are rural women.

Chinese culture emphasizes the common good instead of individual liberty. As a result, political participation and awareness of most people remain very low, especially in the countryside. Under these circumstances, the first step of modernization has to be the development of the economy because it will gradually generate change in other areas. As people's living standards improve, as the nation's education level increases overall, as new social classes and strata form, and as the urbanization rate grows, there will be some ground for stable political change. These changes have, in fact, been occurring in China and will surely continue. Even though the path of change may not be smooth, economic development will promote political development.

Second, the consequences of rapid economic liberalization in the former Soviet Union indicate that China's model of development is more suitable for a country in transition. If China had assumed the same model of development as did the former Soviet Union, the results would have been even worse because the levels of general education, living standards, and gross domestic product were much lower in China than they were in the former Soviet Union. Today, however, Chinese people live much better than the people in the former Soviet Union. China is enjoying economic prosperity while the former Soviet states suffer political and economic turmoil.

Third, a process of gradual change suits the Asian tradition and has frequently been the pattern of political evolution in Asia since the Second World War. In this region, few countries have a true democratic political system in the Western tradition, but most of them have done very well economically. Furthermore, economic success has been accompanied in recent years by demands for more choice and responsiveness in government. Because China is so different from the West in many aspects, it cannot adopt an entirely Western path of development.

A careful examination of the experiences of the developed East Asian countries and regions shows a striking similarity between China's approach and earlier East Asian approaches. Over the past 20 to 40 years, economic reform has had a major impact on political change in the Asian-Pacific region. Within this region, the countries that have been able to create a stable political order in the early and intermediate stages of development have usually been fairly successful in promoting economic development. It is also important to note that those countries with low levels of economic development, with a few exceptions, tend to have authoritarian regimes, while those with high levels of economic development tend to have more democratic governments. Economic development will surely promote political development. I emphasize *promote* because political change will not happen automatically. The real challenge of economic reform, therefore, is political development.

Most Chinese scholars believe that the path of China's reform reflects a political logic. There is no doubt that freedom and democracy are the common aspirations of mankind. There is also no doubt that a complete package of human rights is part of a higher standard of civilization. The question here is how to achieve them. The different backgrounds and historical conditions of different countries and regions in the world mean that there will inevitably be different routes to approach the same goal. Western democratic political institutions were usually established before overall economic development because Western historical conditions are different.

In contrast, Asian countries do not have this kind of historical background. Asian countries generally cannot follow the route of political evolution taken by Western countries. For example, by the late 1980s, the pressure of economic growth had led South Korea and Taiwan to democratize. Because their economic development had already taken place, their transition to democracy was smooth. The pressure for transition and democracy in Asian countries must come from inside the states; otherwise, it will not work.

Fourth, China's gradual model of development is not only in the interest of the Chinese people but also conforms to the interests of people all over the world, including people in the West. It is obvious that a stable and prosperous China will serve the interests of peace and stability better than an unstable and chaotic China. China's population is so large that instability within China would surely have a great impact on Asia and the rest of the world. A stable China is therefore in everyone's interest. Furthermore, China's economic reform and development will have a positive impact on the world through the reduction of the price of labor and increased trade in the world's largest and most dynamic markets. The Chinese market has a potential 1.2 billion consumers.

Development policy emphasizes the gradual introduction of reform, as opposed to the introduction of reform as a comprehensive package. The aim has been to transform the economy not by abolishing central planning completely, but by allowing markets and nonstate firms to grow outside of the traditional planned economy. Gradualism is the key to China's success, for it suits China's reality and has protected the nation from turmoil.

Another characteristic of China's reform is its use of experimentation. "Cross the river by feeling the stones" vividly expresses China's views of reform. What has worked here has not been a whole package of reasoned and calculated development, but rather a series of "one-step-forward" experiments and bold, new practices. The development of household contracts in rural areas, the establishment of special economic zones, and the adoption of a dual-price system are some of the bold initiatives that were taken at the beginning of the reform process. The "shareholding" method to reform state-owned enterprises will be the next experiment in this process. The shareholding company is regarded as a model for state sector transformation because it is easy for the state through this method to transfer its assets to individuals. In addition, an increasing number of semiprivate companies—that is, those that allow the government to keep a smaller stake in the equity—have recently emerged. These companies are usually well managed and extremely active in China's business world.

One should remember, however, that China still can (and should) draw on some lessons from Western political development. I do not agree with the point of view that China's political development can be built solely upon Confucianism. The fast-developing East Asian countries have, in fact, drawn on the experiences of Western democratic systems during the course of their democratic transition. China should adopt what is appropriate from Western experiences and combine that knowledge with China's unique cultural heritage.

IV. Problems and Solutions

The path of reform and development has not been and will not be smooth for China; reformers have faced many challenges. Currently, the two biggest problems facing China's population are inflation and corruption. China's annual nationwide inflation rate last year reached 13 percent, but the inflation rate of the major cities peaked at 22 percent. The government's target is to keep the inflation rate within 10 percent for 1994, even though it has never been higher than 20 percent and is much lower than that of the former Soviet Union and Eastern European countries. The states of the former Soviet Union experienced a 91 percent inflation rate in 1991 and a 2,000 percent inflation rate in 1992. Nevertheless, China still has to deal with the problem and ease public fears of rampant inflation.

Second, corruption has resulted from the emergence of the market economy, which brought with it special opportunities for local government officials to use their social connections for exploitation of the marketplace and become the special profiteers of the new market economy. During recent years, there have been many cases of corruption among local officials, which has resulted in a growing discontent among the masses. In general, however, the incidence of corruption during the development process is not that unusual. Many East Asian countries also experienced corruption scandals during their economic transition periods. The lesson from the Asian developmental experience is that if the government can maintain control and push the country through to a largely market economy, then the discipline that competition requires will force businesses that are too corrupt out of the market. China's government has put considerable effort into tackling the corruption problem, already with some success.

The final solution of the problem rests upon the development of a relatively modern legal system. Business necessity and popular demand are forces pushing for the development of such a system. Currently, China lacks a complete legal framework and a law enforcement system, which is necessary for a smoothly functioning market economy. China's foreign investors are calling for the creation of a modern legal system with binding contracts, property rights, and courts to adjudicate disputes. The drive for the rule of law is greatest among active players in the market economy, for once a relatively modern legal system is established, corruption will wane.

QUESTION: Was the population of each household substantially the same in 1992 as it was in 1978?

MS. WANG: It was almost the same. China's birth control policy allows a family only one child. In the cities, the policy works very well, but it does not work very well in the countryside. In the cities, almost every family has one child, but in the countryside, the families still tend to be large because the household contract system requires labor, and more family members means more labor.

Substantial progress has been made in the rural areas and people have recognized and welcomed economic reform there. Rural living standards have increased because people work harder. Public lands have been contracted to peasants, but it is almost as if the land belongs to them, for peasants can use the land in any way they choose. Eight hundred million peasants have been relatively freed from state control. These people can now do any work they choose in any place, including in the cities.

QUESTION: Though China's progress has been great, at some point in the developmental process, the economy is going to run into resistance from the bureaucracy. At what point of China's development do you think economic development will meet with bureaucratic resistance? At what point will the bureaucracy begin to negatively impact the economy?

MS. WANG: China's economic development is not likely to meet with bureaucratic resistance in the near future. Decentralization is essential to China's economic development and its position as a regional competitor.

QUESTION: I have a question about factory wages and the freedom of factory managers to set wages and working conditions.

I spent six months in China four years ago surveying the textile industry and factories. In the factories that I surveyed, the staffing was set by the bureaucracy outside the factory. I recommended that factories reduce their staffing by a substantial proportion, and the factory managers responded by saying that they could not do that because the staffing was set by the government. They also indicated that wages were preset and that factory workers had no freedom to move between factories. To what degree has that changed?

MS. WANG: It has changed a great deal. Earlier in China, the work unit strictly controlled the people. The work unit controlled everything, including housing and salary, freedom to travel, and even marriage. Now that an increasing number of collective and private enterprises are established, many people have left these public government work units to have businesses of their own. They work in private enterprises, collective enterprises, and even foreign companies. Individuals are now totally free to make these changes. Factory managers now also have some latitude to set wages in their own factories. They are more flexible than before.

QUESTION: When I was there, people were making the equivalent of 24 cents an hour. Are wages still so low?

MS. WANG: Although wages are not as low now, they still tend to be relatively low. China has attracted a great deal of foreign investment, in part due to cheap labor.

QUESTION: Is it true that certain sections of China are improving much faster than others?

MS. WANG: Yes, the situation in some areas, especially some coastal areas and Shenzhen, have a much better situation. Some remote areas in the mountains are far worse. Significant disparities exist, and they are getting larger and larger.

In very poor areas, there is little difference in people's standard of living. If you worked in a factory, or if you were a professor, your living standard was about the same. Today,

166

however, the difference in the standard of living between two such occupations is increasing.

COMMENT: Your comment that resources have been transferred to those with lower position and power during the reform era is interesting. To some extent, I understand how resources would be transferred to those of lower position and power, but I would think that more well-connected people would have better access to these resources.

MS. WANG: The cases to which you refer are the corruption cases, but generally the people who benefited most from the reforms were the people in the lower positions—the lower status people. This is especially true of people living in the countryside. Thus, for this reason the nation as a whole has welcomed economic reform.

NARRATOR: Thank you, Professor Wang, for your informative discussion.

IV

CHINA AND BEYOND

CHAPTER TEN

The New World Order and Taiwan's Emerging International Role*

Cheng-yi Lin

NARRATOR: Professor S. C. Leng, who is in charge of our Asian Studies Program, will introduce today's speaker.

MR. LENG: Dr. Cheng-yi Lin was one of our star students at the University of Virginia, from which he received his doctorate. He received support from some of the most prominent foundations in the world while he was a student here. Presently he is an associate research fellow at the Institute of European and American Studies at the Academia Sinica, the most prestigious research institute in Asia. He has also written a number of books. It is my pleasure to present Dr. Lin to you.

MR. LIN: I am delighted to share my recent research on Taiwan's political development and its future foreign policy outlook. In the analysis of a country's foreign policy, three dimensions must be considered: 1) the decisionmakers; 2) the internal structure of the state or the domestic government; and 3) the international system.

---

*Presented in a Forum at the Miller Center of Public Affairs on 20 September 1993.

Proceeding from this three-dimensional framework, it is evident that from 1949 to 1971 both Taiwan's decisionmaker—President Chiang Kai-shek—and its domestic government were very dogmatic. The international system at that time was shaped in large part by U.S. containment policy toward the People's Republic of China (PRC)—or Communist China. Though the People's Republic of China controlled more territory and had a much larger population, the Republic of China (ROC or Taiwan) was the one that occupied China's permanent seat on the United Nations Security Council. In 1971, however, the Republic of China was replaced by the PRC in the United Nations and in most other specialized U.N. organizations. From 1971 to 1972, most of the major players in the international society discontinued their recognition of Taiwan and cut off diplomatic relations with it, leaving only approximately 22 countries who continued to recognize the Republic of China during the remainder of the 1970s.

Beginning in 1988, however, when President Lee Teng-hui succeeded Chiang Ching-Kuo and as the leaders became better educated and more pragmatic, the political agenda and stance of Taiwan's decisionmakers began to change. Domestically, Taiwan's government is no longer a dictatorship; it is now a democratic government with a two-party system. As Joseph S. Nye, Jr. has explained, the post-Cold War era is characterized by a multilevel-interdependent structure, which has had both positive and negative impacts on Taiwan's security and foreign policy outlook. While the top layer of military power is largely unipolar because there is no other state comparable to the United States in that arena, the middle layer of economic power is tripolar, composed of the United States, Japan, and Western Europe. Finally, the bottom layer of transitional interdependence shows a diffusion of power.

According to President George Bush's speech before a joint session of Congress on 11 September 1990, one objective of the United States—which had become the sole superpower, leading the grand alliance against Saddam Hussein—during the Persian Gulf conflict was to establish "a new world order," in which states could be "freer from the threat of terror, stronger in the pursuit of justice, are more secure in the quest for peace." George Bush went further to say that in this new world order, "the rule of law supplants the

172

rule of the jungle, a world in which nations recognize the shared responsibility for freedom and justice, a world where the stronger respect the rights of the weak." George Bush summarized the principles of the new world order as follows: "peaceful settlements of disputes, solidarity against aggression, reduced and controlled arsenals, and just treatment of all people." He also called for "a new partnership based on consultation, cooperation, and collective action, especially through international and regional organization."

Charles Krauthammer once argued that the end of the Cold War marked the beginning of Pax Americana, or a unipolar moment for international society. The United States, however, occupies a less than commanding role in the international economy, demonstrated by the fact that countries such as Japan, Germany, Kuwait, and Saudi Arabia paid nearly the entire bill for the Persian Gulf War.

The end of the Cold War has not brought peace and stability to East Asia. First, the diminishing U.S. military presence has caused a reactive military buildup in the region. President Lee Teng-hui noted that the gradual U.S. military pullout from Asia may have a strong impact on the region's stability and cautioned against Beijing's military buildup and Japan's adoption of a bill providing for an overseas peacekeeping force. To President Lee, a new security system to maintain peace in the region is imperative. His observation is echoed by Defense Minister Sun Chen, who argues that Beijing is creating instability in the region through its military buildup and its attempt to become a regional superpower. Second, four out of the five remaining socialist countries are in East Asia—North Korea, China, Vietnam, and Laos—and these regimes are potential threats to the region. For example, North Korea's secret nuclear program, the number-one threat to stability in the Asia-Pacific region, could trigger nuclear proliferation to Japan, Taiwan, and South Korea. Third, confidence and security-building measures, such as the Conference on Security and Cooperation in Europe (CSCE), that would alleviate such pressures are absent in East Asia. Given the enduring security environment of the region, Fredrick Chien, Taiwan's foreign minister, has argued that the Cold War structure remains largely intact in East Asia, and furthermore, the Republic of China remains an outsider to the emerging international order.

Taiwan's abnormal international status. Figures show that Taiwan's per capita income is the 25th highest in the world and its gross national product (GNP) ranks 20th globally. Taiwan is the 14th largest global trading nation and it ranks seventh in total overseas investment. Taiwan also has the largest foreign exchange reserves in the world. Despite its prosperous economy, however, Taiwan faces tremendous diplomatic isolation in the international society.

The Republic of China has been struggling to keep its membership in the less than 10 intergovernmental organizations (IGOs) to which it belongs, such as the Asia-Pacific Economic Cooperation conference (APEC) and the Asian Development Bank (ADB). Due to pressure from Beijing, Taiwan is a member of the ADB not under its official name, the Republic of China, but under "Taipei, China." Similarly, its official title was changed to "Chinese Taipei" in APEC.

As I mentioned earlier, there are only 28 countries that still recognize the Republic of China as a sovereign state, most of which are small, obscure mini-states. A few of them are not even members of the United Nations. In contrast, Beijing is recognized by 157 countries. Chinese Communist leaders never hesitate to note that the Taiwanese authorities are only representatives of a local government. According to Beijing's recently published "White Paper on the Taiwan Question and the Reunification of China," Taiwan is not allowed to establish diplomatic relations or aviation services with other countries. It is also not permitted to participate in the United Nations or to acquire its own defensive weapons from the West.

Taiwan's emerging international role. Taiwan's Cold War image as an anti-Communist agent has changed significantly. With the end of the Cold War, Taiwan has become more eager to demonstrate its national power and to pursue a policy that will improve its international image. Taiwan's foreign policy has involved maintaining the balance of power across the Taiwan Straits, a policy term that can have multiple meanings in international politics. For example, it can describe an equilibrium of power distribution among competing states, but it can also refer to a policy that promotes the preservation of that equilibrium.

With the end of the Cold War, Taiwan has succeeded in obtaining contracts of F-16 fighter jets from the United States and Mirage-2000s from France in 1992. Though it is impossible for Taiwan to compete with China in every aspect of military capability, Taiwan believes that further improving its quality of military hardware is the only way to overcome its inferiority in terms of numbers of fighter jets and warships. Taiwan's contemporary military posture is primarily based on issues of self-defense, but it also aims to make the risk and costs of any coercive action by Beijing unbearable for the PRC.

Taiwan has sought to deter China not only by increasing its military power, but also by pooling its resources with other countries that pursue identical policies with regard to China. In fact, some experts believe that Taiwan may have some kind of secret military cooperation with some of the Southeast Asian countries to counterbalance the PRC's expansionism. Although there is no chance of Taiwan establishing a military alliance with any country in the Asia-Pacific region, realists in Taiwan nevertheless are quick to explore the possibility of establishing a buffer zone between China and Taiwan. In May 1990, President Lee Teng-hui called for Beijing's leaders to roll back the People's Liberation Army's (PLA) deployment 300 kilometers from the Fujian Province facing Quemoy and Matsu. The opposition party—the Democratic Progress Party (DPP)—endorsed the idea that Quemoy and Matsu be demilitarized.

A final policy tool increasingly employed by Taiwan has been the method of "divide and rule." As a result of Taiwan's and Hong Kong's growing investment in southern China, particularly in the provinces of Guangdong and Fujian, the per capita GNP in these four regions reached U.S. $4,000 in 1991. Taipei has used this investment as leverage to influence the decision-making process of local governments in southern China. Some circles in Taiwan would like to see this leverage used to foster separatism or military regionalism in China, thus lessening Beijing's military pressure on Taiwan.

Taiwan also sees itself as a supporter of the collective security system. Generally, when a state feels it cannot defend itself, it will look for protection through collective security measures. For example, the Republic of China, though not a member of the United Nations, supported the 12 U.N. resolutions that condemned Iraq for its invasion of Kuwait. In September 1990, Foreign Minister Chien announced that Taipei would contribute U.S. $30 million to Jordan, Turkey, and Egypt, whose economies were affected by the Persian Gulf crisis. It was reported in Taipei that the ROC had proposed to offer U.S. $100 million in assistance to the United States for the Desert Storm operation but was turned down by Washington. It seems strange that a country would turn down money offered to it by another country, but Washington did so in response to political pressure from Beijing.

To a certain extent, Taipei extended its support for U.N. actions against Iraq in the hope that the collective security system would someday help Taiwan to defend itself from any Chinese offensive military actions. President Lee Teng-hui mentioned that the U.N. actions in the Gulf sent "a strong signal to all countries and regimes that aggression will be punished by the international community." In addition to trying to use the United Nations to protect Taiwan, President Lee in recent years has also initiated a proposal to establish a collective security system in the Asia-Pacific region. This proposal includes the establishment of a collective protection fund, an arms control program in Asia, and the joint exploration of natural resources in the South China Sea. Taipei's commitment to building a new Pacific community and its willingness to integrate its efforts with other political units effectively demonstrates Taiwan's emerging role as a regional collaborator.

Taiwan can also be seen as a post-Cold War practitioner of the functional approach to international relations. Functionalists argue that the development of economic and social cooperation between states is a major condition for the ultimate solution of political conflicts. The effect of mutual cooperation in social and economic issues are believed to spill over into the political realm and allow for the settlement of security issues. Not only has functionalism played a role in European integration and been used as an approach by specialized organizations of the United Nations, but it also has been used by Taiwan as an approach to eliminate conflicts with China.

Taiwan has rejected party-to-party talks for reunification as proposed by Beijing, insisting that cultural exchanges must come first, then bilateral trade, and finally political contacts will follow. This idea is reflected in the Guidelines for National Unification adopted by the ROC, which essentially states that Taiwan's reunification policy is a policy of "one China, but not now."

Despite the lack of official contacts between Taiwan and China, the two countries have been engaged in informal relations since 1987 through tourism and economic, cultural, and sports exchanges, all of which are increasing rapidly. An average of one million Taiwan residents visit the mainland every year. Bilateral indirect trade through Hong Kong was U.S. $1.5 billion in 1987 and reached U.S. $8.6 billion in 1993. Taiwan's investment on the mainland is estimated to be U.S. $10 billion. In the absence of official contacts, a private but government-endorsed Straits Exchange Foundation (SEF) was established by the ROC government to handle bilateral trade problems with the Chinese mainland. Beijing also set up a counterpart organization, the Association for Relations across the Taiwan Straits (ARATS) to increase contacts with Taiwan.

In April 1993, the first high-level semiofficial meeting between the chairmen of these two organizations—Koo Chen-fu, the chairman of Taiwan's SEF, and Wang Daohan, chairman of China's ARATS—was held in Singapore. The Koo-Wang meeting was described by Taipei as "nongovernmental, economic, and functional in nature." Altogether, four agreements were signed between China and Taiwan. One of the agreements dealt with cross-strait educational, cultural, and scientific exchanges as well as the joint exploitation of natural resources. These agreements are illustrative of Taiwan's functional approach toward the achievement of peace and security for Taiwan.

Taiwan's emerging role as a developer—a term I use here to mean a state with a special obligation to assist developing countries—has been impressive in recent years. Growing economic prosperity has worked to Taipei's advantage by making more funds available for Taiwan's foreign aid packages. In 1988, Taipei established an International Economic Cooperation and Development Fund and appropriated U.S. $1.2 billion of foreign aid to

Third World countries. Today, Taiwan has dispatched 43 teams of technical experts to 31 countries. Taiwan has even set a goal to raise its foreign aid to 0.15 percent of its GNP.

Taiwan's foreign investments in most of the Southeast Asian countries occupy an important rank in the list of major foreign investors. As of 1992, Taiwan's investment in Southeast Asia has amounted to U.S. $15 billion. Through this investment channel, Taipei has increased political and military contact with Southeast Asian countries and has successfully achieved investment guarantee agreements with all ASEAN (Association of Southeast Asian nations) countries except Brunei. At the same time, however, Taipei's aim to become a ASEAN dialogue partner has yet to be realized.

To conclude, economic elements of national power such as economic growth and trade have become increasingly important in the new world order, and as a result, Taiwan has found it easier to demonstrate its power in international society. At the same time, however, Taiwan, even with its population of 21 million—which is greater than that of two-thirds of the U.N. members—is still kept outside of the United Nations and its specialized organizations.

Taiwan will have to fight a hard battle if it is to gain membership to the United Nations. As global trends continue toward democratization, development, and détente in the post-Cold War period and as democratization takes root in Taiwan, Taipei is looking forward to making a greater contribution to the new world order and is likely to pursue U.N. membership more actively, as the people of the island will definitely not stand by and watch their future be determined single-handedly by the PRC.

QUESTION: How much is Taiwan's current political predicament the result of President Truman's and Dean Acheson's decision to not make Taiwan an independent entity following its liberation from the Japanese?

MR. LIN: Some international lawyers still support that argument, but I would point out that from 1949 to 1971, under the support of the United States, most countries recognized the tiny Republic of China, not the very large Communist China. After 1971, however, this situation reversed. Some people in Taiwan currently argue that Taiwan should be independent from Communist China because the PRC never exercised its sovereignty over the island. It is significant that Beijing both claims sovereignty over the island and insists that Taiwan should not participate in any official international organizations. Beijing has attempted to make Taiwan into a territory like Hong Kong, which will become one of the PRC's locally governed territories in the future.

COMMENT: It strikes me that Taiwan must find the United States rather unreliable and that the United States, in its own interest, should support and protect such a prosperous, energetic nation. The United States probably would not let Taiwan be overrun, but it is certainly hard to predict what the United States might do if the mainland attacked Taiwan. The situation is unfortunate, but at least no one has started dropping bombs.

MR. LIN: In 1990 when Iraq invaded Kuwait, some people in Taiwan discussed the possibility of a similar situation emerging between Taiwan and the People's Republic of China. Some people even suggested that Taiwan might become a second Israel. I believe, however, that Taiwan must depend on itself first before depending on others.

In the Taiwan Relations Act, the U.S. government mentioned that it would not sit idle if there were an invasion by Communist China. The United States, however, could respond in a number of ways to fulfill that promise. Rather than send in military troops to defend Taiwan, the United States could just sell Taiwan a defensive weapons system. In this respect, Taiwan is still dependent on the United States and Western Europe; that is, Taiwan's acquisition of a sophisticated defensive military system would depend on the supply of equipment from those countries. The United States could also respond to an invasion of Taiwan by issuing a policy statement warning the Beijing government not to take any military action against Taiwan, or it could increase its military presence in the Asia-Pacific region. It seems to me that it is better for the United States to deter a PRC invasion before it happens than to send military troops to the region afterward.

QUESTION: Regarding the defense of Taiwan, has there been any discussion of the United States setting up bases in Taiwan to replace the two bases it lost in the Philippines?

MR. LIN: The government of the United States does not have any diplomatic relations with Taiwan. It would be a sensitive issue to maintain U.S. military bases on Taiwan or to have any political contact between officials in the State Department and their counterparts in Taiwan. After the U.S. withdrawal from Subic Bay and Clark Air Force Base, it was argued that Taiwan should welcome a U.S. military base on Taiwan, but I do not think that will be possible.

Despite the closing of U.S. bases in the Philippines, the United States still maintains a military presence in the regions of Indonesia, Thailand, and Malaysia under agreements that allow the United States to use the facilities of these countries for logistical support. Yet because of its relations with China, the United States would find it difficult to have any direct military relations with Taiwan concerning defensive weapons.

QUESTION: What is the population of Taiwan in relation to that of the People's Republic of China?

MR. LIN: The population in Taiwan is about 21 million, and the population of mainland China is roughly 1.1 billion, about 25 percent of the world's population.

QUESTION: Do you know what the sentiments of those billion people are with respect to the aspirations of Taiwan?

MR. LIN: It is difficult to predict the future of Taiwan. Many Taiwanese have immigrated to places such as Canada and the United States because of the uncertainty regarding Chinese public opinion of the issue of Taiwan. The possibility that Taiwan might become a second Hong Kong is a growing concern in Taiwan. Taiwan has attempted to promote mainland China's peaceful evolution by increasing investment in the PRC, by endeavoring to improve the living standards of the Chinese people on the mainland,

and by trying to change the PRC's socialist system into a democratic one. It is likely, however, that the process of a peaceful evolution will take a long time, perhaps 40 or 50 years. Given the uncertainty of Taiwan's future, many people in Taiwan have taken precautionary measures, such as investing overseas and in China or acquiring a second passport from another country so that if China takes any action against Taiwan, they will be able to leave quickly.

QUESTION: It is my impression that the political differences between Taiwan and the mainland were much sharper during the early years when the Guomindang and Chiang Kai-shek first arrived in Taiwan than they are now. Today there is more dialogue between the two on the division of political administration and economic philosophy. Is it not true that the successful economic policies in Taiwan are being followed by economic activities in China designed to promote a future trend toward commercial interchange that may make it economically advantageous for mainland China to have a more tolerant attitude toward Taiwan?

MR. LIN: Some people, particularly the local Taiwanese, want Taiwan to declare *de jure* independence from China. Beijing, however, has frequently indicated that it would consider taking military action against Taiwan if Taiwan were to declare itself to be an independent country. As a result of their differing positions on the issue, Taiwan and mainland China are neither friends nor enemies.

Thus, Taiwan's international status continues to be a strange one. Though Taiwan can go to the Chinese mainland and talk to Chinese Communist leaders such as President Jiang Zemin and have dinner with them, in certain other arenas such as international organizations, Beijing will not allow Taiwan to have a separate status. Beijing also will not allow any country to have official relations with the Republic of China because, as Beijing claims, there is only one China—the People's Republic of China—and therefore the ROC is only a local government whose status should be like that of Hong Kong.

The people of Taiwan are not satisfied anymore with the current arrangement. They want to exercise their economic power, but they also want to exercise their political power, particularly their representation in international society. Some people even ridicule Taiwan because it always pays money under the table yet can never sit at the table. Taiwan's situation is truly unique; I cannot think of any other country in the world that has experienced the diplomatic isolation that Taiwan has, except maybe the Palestinian Liberation Organization (PLO), which is now enjoying mutual recognition with Israel. Taiwan, however, is not recognized as a major player in international society, and as I already mentioned, only very tiny states recognize Taiwan.

QUESTION: Regarding the threats to Asian stability that you mentioned—for example the lack of strong regional economic structures and the U.S. military withdrawal from the Asia-Pacific region—how do you see the role of ASEAN countries fulfilling the void in both security and economic matters? Also, what will be the character of future relations between Taiwan and ASEAN?

MR. LIN: In 1967 when ASEAN was first established, it was designed to facilitate economic cooperation among its members. Approximately two years ago, the ASEAN also began to include military consultations under its framework as a result of a growing sense of threat from China. Though members have diplomatic relations with the People's Republic of China, ASEAN countries nevertheless wanted the United States to stay in East Asia, so they opened their facilities and welcomed the U.S. military presence in the region.

Taiwan has applied for membership to ASEAN many times but has always been turned down. The ASEAN countries have "dialogue" partners such as the United States, Japan, South Korea, and the West European community. Taiwan ought to try to become one of ASEAN's dialogue partners, even though there are no official relations between members of the ASEAN and Taiwan, and establish other types of relationships with these states. For example, Singapore, which is a member of ASEAN, sent its troops to Taiwan because being a tiny island, it does not have many military facilities of its own. Taiwan, however, does and can provide Singapore with such facilities.

It is difficult to say what will be the future of relations between ASEAN and Taiwan, but there is no doubt in my mind that the ASEAN countries would not support Taiwan militarily if China were to attack Taiwan. They might, however, issue policy statements in support of the United States if the U.S. government were to give its support to Taiwan.

MR. BRANTLY WOMACK: Over the last four or five years, I have been much more optimistic about relations between Taiwan and the mainland not because Taiwan's defensive capabilities have increased, but because the chances of military conflict have diminished. Your discussion includes many of Taiwan's options in the event of a military attack by the mainland, but I have not seen any evidence in the 1980s that such an attack is likely. I do not see anything in the near or intermediate term that would make that possibility realistic.

On the other hand, there are a couple of things that do worry me about your discussion on future relations between Taiwan and China. Both the PRC and the ROC claim sovereignty over the same territory, but only one sovereign government can be recognized over a given territory. Therefore, if we talk about the Republic of China and the People's Republic of China, then your earlier point of why states have not recognized the Republic of China becomes moot.

Getting back to an earlier point of yours, another thing that disturbed me was that you said Taiwan was planning to use its $10 billion investment in southern China as leverage within Chinese politics, particularly to support Chinese separatism and regionalism. If you are speaking for Taiwan or even a significant part of the population of Taiwan, aren't you contemplating what can be considered as aggressive action against the current government of China? If you are saying that Taiwan would support a military leadership in Guangdong that declared its independence from the Communist government, wouldn't they then still be fighting a kind of cold war? Aren't you still considering the government in Beijing the enemy and saying that the battle is not over; the war is not lost; we are not in a new situation, this is just a different phase of the war? What you say concerns me because first of all, I do not think it is feasible, and the unity of mainland China is unlikely to dissolve into regionalism. Second, I think that regionalism would be the most dangerous thing that could happen in the Pacific, for Taiwan especially.

That gets back to a previous question raised regarding what China's one billion people think. I think that the PRC's one billion people have nothing against Taiwan, and certainly they have nothing against the people in Taiwan. Nevertheless, the one billion people do think of Taiwan as part of China, and it will be hard to convince them otherwise.

MR. LIN: I do agree that military confrontation between Taiwan and China is unlikely, but only so long as Taiwan does not declare its independence. As I mentioned before, Beijing has stated that a declaration of independence from Taiwan would be met with military action. Furthermore, Taiwan has a two-party system, and by the year 2000 there will have been two presidential elections. It is therefore difficult to predict whether the ruling Guomindang will remain the ruling party or become the opposition party before the year 2000. If the DPP declares Taiwan's independence, it is possible that Taiwan will be under attack or be subject to military coercion. Thus, military confrontation is unlikely, since the possibility that this one precondition will occur is unlikely.

Many people say that Taiwan does not need a defensive weapons system, but I should mention that all of the other countries in the Asia-Pacific region such as Japan, South Korea, Indonesia, and Singapore have F-15s or F-16s. In 1992 the United States and France sold sophisticated fighter jets to Taiwan, which may have been the last country in the region to get the F-16s. Malaysia even got F-18s from the United States recently. Taiwan, therefore, has to build up or even implement a military modernization program.

Regarding the second part of your question, I am not speaking for the Taiwanese government. I am merely pointing out that there are some circles in Taiwan that would like to see separatism or military regionalism in China and thus see the political leadership in Beijing weakened. These circles believe that Taiwan's capital investments in China's southern regions will have some influence and cause military regions in the south to think twice about the risks of taking military action against Taiwan should Beijing give the order to do so. You may be right in saying that such thinking is dangerous. Nevertheless, relations between Taiwan and China remain very strange. Neither friends nor enemies, they can talk like friends and toast each other at dinner parties, but in other situations, they are still enemies, despite the end of the Cold War.

QUESTION: John Gaddis wrote a book titled *Strategies of Containment: A Critical Appraisal of Postwar American National Security Policy* (1982). In this book he argues that a country must have the means to meet its ends. How does Taiwan fare with regard to this argument?

Also, do you agree with the deputy director of the Center of International Studies who said that the order of priorities for Taiwan at this moment should be first, domestic politics; second, mainland China; third, foreign policies? What is your opinion of a statement made by a Taiwanese professor that Taiwan is practicing so-called rich-boy foreign policy?

MR. LIN: There have been different opinions as to whether Taiwan should apply for membership in the United Nations. There are 184 member states in the United Nations, but only 24 U.N. members have recognized the Republic of China. Perhaps those who say that Taiwan stands no chance of becoming a U.N. member in the near future are right.

The people in Taiwan are divided about the official title they should use when applying for membership in the United Nations. The official title, Republic of China, is only recognized by 28 countries, so many Taiwanese people would prefer to use Taiwan as its official name and not the Republic of China.

Furthermore, people are divided as to whether China should be unified or divided and whether Taiwan should be independent from China. I do not agree with those who say that Taiwan should be satisfied with the current situation. I think Taiwan should apply for U.N. membership, because given the economic power that it has today, Taiwan deserves to be treated as an equal partner or an equal country member by other United Nations members. If Taiwan cannot be satisfied with its international or diplomatic standing, more people will immigrate to other countries, while people in the government of Taiwan will remain unsatisfied with the status quo. The opposition party, in particular, will try to declare Taiwan independent. It is, therefore, risky for Taiwan to continue its current status in international society.

Regarding the earlier question about what people in mainland China think of Taiwan, I think the people on the mainland know about Taiwan's economic development. Although they think that Taiwan should be separate from China, they would side with Beijing in its use of coercive action to prevent Taiwan from declaring its independence.

MR. LENG: As far as U.N. membership is concerned, the only solution is to maintain the status quo and try to obtain observer status for Taiwan in the United Nations. Such an arrangement has the advantage of historical precedence, as divided nations such as South Vietnam, North Vietnam, East Germany, and West Germany have all had separate observers in the United Nations before their unifications. Also, North and South Korea now are separate members in the United Nations because South Korea had no veto power.

In view of China's permanent membership on the U.N. Security Council and hence its veto power, however, it is totally unrealistic, whatever name Taiwan chooses to use, to think that it will become a member without China's consent. Observer status has many advantages, one being that observer status would certainly be much better than being excluded from the United Nations altogether.

As for the independence movement in Taiwan, even Huang Hsin-chieh, the former president of the opposition party who once considered independence to be the primary aim of its party platform, realizes the danger of provoking the PRC.

Assuming that Taiwan does declare its independence, what would the PRC do? Even the opposition party's former leader noted that the PRC would not have to send any troops, but instead fire a few missiles at Taiwan, which would create enough of a psychological impact to cause the collapse of Taiwan's economic prosperity. The best hope for the time being, therefore, is to keep what Taiwan has now and try to improve its international status or, as you said, try to influence peaceful change in China. Taiwan should maintain its divided nation status, which will not preclude either future unification or total separation. Even if the opposition party were to win the presidency in 1996, which I doubt, it is not likely to declare independence because the risk is too great. Taiwan might continue to assert its independence in practical ways, but *de jure* independence for the time being is quite unrealistic and very dangerous.

NARRATOR: We have been privy to a very illuminating discussion and insightful questions. The best route to understanding in this country has always been the exchange of different perspectives and the honest expression of different views. We thank you very much.

CHAPTER ELEVEN

The Empowerment of Asia*

CHALMERS JOHNSON

MR. LENG: Professor Chalmers Johnson is the president of the Japan Policy Research Institute, a nonprofit research and public affairs organization devoted to public education concerning Japan. He first visited Japan in 1953 as a U.S. Navy officer and has lived and worked there virtually every year since 1961. He is currently working on a study of former Japanese Prime Minister Kakuei Tanaka and the problem of structural corruption in the Japanese state.

MR. JOHNSON: I would like to begin by saying a few words about the Japan Policy Research Institute (JPRI). One of our goals is to try to reestablish among educated Americans the need for an understanding of area studies. The contemporary American academy, particularly its social-science wing and its economics and business segments, unfortunately denigrates such knowledge as cultural trivia, anecdotes, mere history, or a preoccupation with esoteric languages. The academy contrasts such knowledge with its own devotion to theory, usually meaning abstractions that involve neither skill nor research. The degree to which Americans today believe that they can get along in the world speaking only English is astonishing.

Presented in a Forum at the Miller Center of Public Affairs on 31 January 1995.

We at JPRI see area studies to mean empirical, inductive country analyses and culturally specific tests of any and all claims to universal truth. There is an enormous demand today in America for information about the world's richest economy, Japan, and the world's fastest growing economy, China, which is also the world's largest social system. People in the United States are so worried about China and Japan that they try to ignore them. China and Japan are the only two nations on earth today that could threaten the national security of the United States, yet there is almost no serious work done on them in the United States.

When first invited to speak at the Miller Center, I was told that the Center was particularly interested in my view of the post-Cold War world, the world that has come into being since the fall of the Berlin Wall in the autumn of 1989 and the implosion of the Soviet Union in the summer of 1991. The primary theme of my presentation is the enormous shift that has taken place in the balance of power in post-Cold War Asia. In the present age, people are simply waiting for an incident to reveal how thoroughly the balance of power has shifted.

Over the past five years there have been three main trends in transpacific international relations. First, Japan's main shapers of public opinion—the bureaucracy, business leaders, journalists, and intellectuals—have been preparing the country for Japan's strategic disengagement from the United States and its recasting of priorities in favor of Asia and perhaps the United Nations. Second, China has been reacting to Japan's enormous economic influence through its own initiatives to balance Japan's power and efforts to exert its own economic influence among the overseas Chinese and non-Asian investors. Third, there has been the rather palpably obvious drift in American policy, reflecting both inertia after the Cold War with regard to military deployments and expediency in day-to-day policy, depending on domestic political considerations.

As these forces work their way into the consciousness of the peoples of Pacific Asia, the concrete pattern of relations is one of waiting for some incident that will make the intrinsic situation extrinsic. Such an incident would reveal how much the global balance of power has shifted in favor of Asia and how little prepared the Americans are for coping with this development.

Until this catalytic event actually occurs, people will not know for certain what that event will actually be. At one point, it was thought that the catalytic event might be the accumulation of nuclear weapons in North Korea. At another point, Americans thought this catalytic event might be an American pilot, who did not know where he was or what he was doing, drifting across the most dangerous border on earth right now (the 38th Parallel in Korea) and getting himself killed. We are simply waiting for such an event to take place. Until it occurs, what passes for strategic thought is largely public relations posturing, bureaucratic infighting over turf, and the pretense of competence by political officials of the main Pacific powers.

Samuel Huntington's now rather notorious article "The Clash of Civilizations," published in *Foreign Affairs* in the summer of 1993, is a good example of the mixing of ideological opportunism and analysis in its treatment of post-Cold War Asia. Huntington, a professor of politics at Harvard, contends that future wars and global tensions will no longer be based on conflict among states but on clashing civilizations—those broad cultural entities defined by history, language, ethnicity, and religion. Huntington claims to be searching for a framework that will capture and simplify the next phase of world politics just as the Cold War did for the past half-century.

According to Huntington, there are seven or eight of what he calls contending civilizations. These are Western, Confucian, Japanese (note that Japan is the only nation coterminous with a civilization on this list), Islamic, Hindu, Slavic Orthodox, Latin American, and possibly African. Huntington says that each is marked by different understandings of the relationships between citizen and state, freedom and authority, parents and children, and gods or God and human beings.

Some East Asians, notably the outspoken leaders of Singapore, entirely agree with this analysis and find it a convenient explanation for why they commit human rights violations against their own citizens, why tropical rain forests in neighboring countries are destroyed to make toothpicks and chopsticks for Northeast Asian restaurants, and why such practices should not be subject to criticism by outsiders. I should hasten to add that I have been a lecturer at the University of Singapore and that I find the place fascinating. Singapore is the world's most successful fascist society and proud of it. Its very existence contradicts what is taught in universities. It is not supposed to work, but it does so very well.

Huntington's analysis contains problems, however. First, he knows next to nothing about the civilizations he has identified. Fouad Ajami, for example, has written a now-famous and stinging critique of Huntington's characterization of and assumptions about the Islamic world. Second, and of particular interest to many people, his characterization of China and Japan as belonging to different civilizations may stem not so much from ignorance as the intent to cause trouble. The American establishment is deeply threatened by Japan's growing economic power. It is even more threatened by the way in which Japan got that power; namely, its state-directed means of achieving it. Japan offers an example of state-guided capitalism in which the state plays an indispensable role. The real contrast between Japan and the United States, which is becoming more palpable every day, is governmental effectiveness, particularly with regard to economic issues.

Japan's economy is twice the size of Germany's and three-fifths the size of the United States'. Many people in the United States are not sure about how it is governed. Nevertheless, until recently the American establishment tried to explain and deal with Japan by arguing that it was an unthreatening part of the West or that it was converging with the West, reminiscent of the way that the Nazis during World War II and the South Africans under apartheid defined the Japanese as "honorary whites." For example, this is what Francis Fukuyama's "end of history" thesis does indirectly—that is, make Japan a part of liberalism, which is what rational choice theorists in economics and political science departments in English-speaking countries also try to do.

Officially and ideologically, there have been only two explanations for Japan's wealth. One is that the Japanese are clones of Americans; that is, they are in the process of becoming like Americans, and their economy will soon evolve to look like ours. The other is that they are toying with socialism, and Japan will soon collapse. As it turns out, neither is true. Japan is simply based on a different kind of capitalist system. Moreover, everyone else on earth is trying to emulate Japanese, not American, capitalism.

By defining Japan as a separate civilization—that is, separating Japanese civilization from Confucian, or in other words, Chinese civilization—Huntington may have another goal: to lay the intellectual groundwork for his belief that China and Japan are likely to struggle for supremacy in Asia. Also, Huntington believes that this potential conflict will work to both the economic and strategic advantage of the United States. Huntington fails to consider the real possibility that China and Japan will find it more profitable to cooperate, which would be to the possible disadvantage of the United States.

Huntington's analytic framework defines Korea as a part of the Confucian Chinese camp, even though South Korea's infrastructure and development strategy owe a great deal more to Japan than to China. South Korea is also a democracy, which actually places it closer to Western civilization than he suggests. As for Southeast Asia, Huntington is unable to deal with those countries at all since he considers them either of the "Malay subdivision of Islam" or "a part of Greater China," but not as an independent entity.

If Huntington seems more ideological and opportunistic than analytical, what are some alternative approaches to assessing the main trends in post-Cold War international politics? One that I find useful but will ultimately criticize because it is too abstract is the interconnection between the two most obvious empirical developments that have taken place in the wake of the Cold War. These two developments are transnational economic integration—namely, the European Union (EU) and the North American Free Trade Agreement (NAFTA)—and subnational ethnic fragmentation. The economists (I am an ex-economist) love the first but deplore the second, as is obvious from the Bosnian example. Our research leads us to believe that one is causing the other; that is, if one likes Merrill Lynch, he or she should love Bosnia. Though these two developments are related, the relationship is fairly abstract.

Transnational economic integration is caused by the spread of technology, the validation of some form of capitalism by the outcome of the Cold War, the shift from the primacy of military power to economic power, and the impact of the East Asian developmental model on the rest of the world. It takes the form of new regional markets, the European Union, NAFTA, the Association of Southeast Asian Nations (ASEAN) Free Trade Agreement, as well as so-called borderless economies and strategic alliances among companies, multinational corporations, the global telecommunications networks, and the wired world of capital flows from one market to another. Economists, in particular, believe that this integration contributes to the unification of the world and that it is therefore an unqualified good. Transnational economic integration quite specifically transcends civilizations and therefore conflicts with Huntington's prediction; that is, it is possible to belong to quite different civilizations and still enjoy each other if one is out to make money. For example, it is palpably clear that Singapore is a different civilization than ours, but it is certainly a part of the global world of multinational corporations.

The second trend is toward social fragmentation; that is, big countries such as the former Soviet Union, former Czechoslovakia, and former Yugoslavia becoming little ones. Fragmentation also involves a sharp rise in the politicization of ethnicity in most parts of the world, leading to what some have called retribalization. Examples include the Serbian campaigns of ethnic cleansing against their former Muslim and Croat fellow citizens, communal warfare from Azerbaijan to Georgia in southern Russia, attacks by Hindus against Sikhs and Muslims in many parts of India, tribal warfare in South Africa and Rwanda, and Islamic fundamentalism in several Muslim nations. Georgie Anne Geyer has called this trend "the death of citizenship," a malady seen in the United States in the Los Angeles riots of April 1992. I live near Los Angeles, and I guarantee that people fighting in the streets there did not regard each other as fellow citizens.

At some highly abstract level, these two trends are interrelated through their combined effects on the state. The end of the Cold War has created a crisis for the old state system and its particular distribution of sovereignty, a point about which Huntington is analytically prescient. He is right to say that the old state system is in decline, even if he is wrong in his scheme of clashing civilizations.

At the same time that old borders are coming down, which promotes integration, new ones are being built, which leads to fragmentation. Transnational economic ties weaken the commitment of citizens to a particular state and, in Ben Anderson's terms, replace the imagined community of the nation with a different imaged community of producers and consumers. From the point of view of an organized political community, economic interests unite what should not be united: citizens and foreigners. If the term *state* means anything at all, it should include an economic dimension. As a result, the weakening of solidarity based on nationality brings into focus how nationality has helped make invisible the divisions within a community based on ethnicity, race, religion, social class, locality, language, or any other marker that can potentially be politicized. Transnational economic relations thus increase the interconnections of hitherto separate groups but at the same time diminish the political solidarity of previously united peoples. This is one of the interesting things about Japan, for example. Japan today is a near-perfect example of a nation combined with a state. At times, it appears as if Japan's strategy is to wait for their competitors to fall apart and disintegrate, while the Japanese continue to hold themselves together.

Several implications follow these trends. One is that the powerful movements toward economic regionalism are generating at once two equally powerful counterreactions: fear of the strongest partner and fear of being left out. Europeans, for example, fear German dominance. Similarly, Latin America fears U.S. dominance, and East Asians fear Japanese dominance. As a friend in Latin America said to me recently, the world would be a much happier place if the Americans would take their vacations in Thailand and the Japanese would take theirs in Ecuador.

These fears have been somewhat moderated in Europe by the European Union and in the Western Hemisphere by NAFTA. In Asia, however, fears are exacerbated by those Japanese who are unable to accept the fact that their previous imperialism in Korea, China, and Southeast Asia was not welcomed by those on the receiving end.

Even within integrated markets like the one being forged by ASEAN, there is fear of Indonesianization because it is the largest partner. Fear of being left out, however, exerts an equally strong pull. For example, East Europeans, Australians, and New

195

Zealanders are enormously fearful of being left out. Australians, in particular, face a dilemma in that they are emotionally part of the Western world but economically part of Asia, and they have to come to grips with that fact. Australia's fear of being left out lies at the heart of its promotion of APEC, the Asia-Pacific Economic Cooperation forum, as opposed to Malaysia's promotion of the EAEC, the East Asian Economic Caucus. The EAEC, which has been promoted in particular by Prime Minister Datuk Seri Mahathir Mohamad of Malaysia, would exclude all of the English-speaking nations—Australia, New Zealand, as well as the United States and Canada—because NAFTA excludes the Asian nations. By Mahathir's reasoning, if NAFTA can cut out Asia, Asia can certainly exclude the West.

There is no way of knowing how this process of integration and fragmentation, of old borders falling and new borders rising, will resolve itself. The United States alone certainly does not have the resources to establish its own hegemonic order. The new political configuration of the world will probably not be known for decades. It is not obvious that the claims of some civilizations will be greater than those of others; nor is it obvious that a new basis for identity will be advanced to replace state-centered claims of allegiance.

In the meantime, high levels of conflict will occur. Those countries in which nation and state come close to coinciding enjoy an advantage over those with polyethnic societies. Some of the near-perfect nation-states such as Japan may find a winning strategy in simply holding themselves together while their competitors disintegrate. Nevertheless, even then it is doubtful that such a strategy—that is, a simple unity—can be successfully extended to create an inevitably heterogeneous empire.

Some aspects of Samuel Huntington's forecast of clashing civilizations, therefore, may prove accurate, except where his formulation seems ideological—for example, his notion of "West against the rest." But even if the weakening of states due to the growth of transnational economic interests is the ultimate cause of increased ethnic conflict, the connection is highly abstract and the analysis is not a good guide to policy.

A better approach to post-Cold War Asia is historical. Such a perspective draws attention to the enrichment and empowerment of Asia as the main trends affecting global politics after the Cold War. What is taking place in East Asia today has parallels to what took place at the beginning of the 20th century—that is, Germany's rise to power and France and Great Britain's inability to adjust. A similar configuration is occurring in the world today—specifically, the rise of Japanese power, and it is not at all clear that the rest of the world is adjusting very well to it, nor is it obvious that Japan will use its power in an exemplary manner.

A historical approach identifies a new center of gravity in international power and recommends a recasting of the balance of power to reflect this development. In this formulation, the enrichment of Asia took place parallel to the Cold War and is, in fact, one of the lasting effects of the Cold War. What the Cold War did was to distract attention away from economic development in Asia just long enough to make Asian ascendancy irreversible. Historians writing about the Cold War may claim that its most important point was to distract people from what was really taking place in the world, which was the fact that East Asia was becoming fabulously wealthy.

In 1960 the Asian economies represented about 4 percent of total world production. Thirty years later they represented a quarter. On the basis of current trends, they will represent a third of the global economy within a decade. Japan's net savings rate continues to average at above a fifth of its GNP, which is about two-and-a-half times that of any other industrialized economy. All of Asia is saving in the 30 percent range. Asia is the main source of long-term capital on earth today. The savings rates, when translated into investment rates, mean that the world balance of economic power will continue to shift to Asia. It also means that low-saving countries, such as the United States, will remain huge importers of capital. This capital will increasingly come from Asians and will be made available on their terms, which will give them leverage in many fields.

One of JPRI's current projects is an evaluation of the economic effects of the Kobe earthquake. Suddenly the Japanese have something else to do with their capital other than to lend it to overconsuming Americans and Mexicans or even potentially deserving Chinese. This change will almost certainly mean a short-term rise in the cost of capital.

What is equally significant is that for the first time, during 1993 Japan's trade surplus with the other countries in East Asia exceeded its trade surplus with the United States. Using Japan's definitions and accounting methods, in 1993 Japan had a surplus with its Asian trading partners of U.S. $53.6 billion compared to U.S. $50.2 billion surplus with the United States. These figures indicate that inter-Asian trade has become more important than trans-Pacific trade. They also suggest that Japan faces an economic imbalance with its immediate neighbors that is potentially more explosive than even its long-term structural imbalance with the United States.

The most important aspect of the post–Cold War Asia-Pacific region is Japan's growing economic dominance and the degree to which it is integrating the nations in that area. The means of integration are trade, direct investment, aid, financial services, technology transfer, and the example of Japan as an inspiration for an Asian model of development. In general the Asian nations, particularly China, depend on Japan for loans, technology, investment, and foreign aid.

In comparison, they depend on the United States for three things—as a military counterweight to Japan and China, as a consumer market for goods manufactured in Asia, and oddly enough, for higher education. Despite their increasingly shrill claims of having a different civilization from the West, the elites of Asia still send their young adults to the United States for university and graduate education. In fact, the prime minister of Spain, Mr. Fillipe Gonzalez, told me that he regarded American universities to be one of the truly great assets of the United States, but it was upsetting that Americans paid so little attention to them. The prime minister was from Madrid and did not think Americans were taking very good care of their universities in general and the University of California in particular.

Asian dependencies on the United States will change markedly within a decade. Whether the shift will occur in accordance with carefully examined policies or violently, like tectonic plates crashing into each other, is perhaps the main variable in considering the prospects for peace and stability in the region and globally. At present, none of the trends provide grounds for optimism.

The enrichment of Asia is essentially a process that occurred during the Cold War and depended to one degree or another on the opportunities made available by Cold War conditions. The empowerment of Asia, however, is a process with a much longer history. Seen in highly schematic terms, the 19th century was the time of the victimization of Asia. In China, this took the form of the unequal treaties imposed by Western imperialists. In the rest of Asia, except for the buffer state of Thailand, this took the form of European, American, and Japanese colonialism. The 20th century was the time of Asia's revolt against this imperialism: the Chinese Revolution, the biggest revolution among all of the known cases; inter-imperialist wars that gave subject peoples the opportunity to revolt; and wars of national liberation in Indonesia, Indochina, and Malaya. These wars are now over and only a few embers from them still smolder.

The U.S. government may be very slow in extending diplomatic recognition to Vietnam, but rich Americans are beginning to take luxury cruise tours there, just as they have been going to China for the past decade. One tour company now takes Americans to Da Nang, puts them in buses, and takes them for the three-hour drive to Hue. I regard this as a sign that the war is finally over.

There is also the soon-to-change status of Hong Kong. In less than a thousand days, the world's third largest financial center, after London and New York but ahead of Zurich, will be turned over to some of the most ideological people on earth, the Chinese Communists, and there is nothing that can be done about it. Probably the greatest single failure of my field was the advice given to Margaret Thatcher. Typical of Western economists, they convinced Mrs. Thatcher during her 1982 negotiations with Deng Xiaoping over the future of Hong Kong that all of the economic indicators in the world suggested that Hong Kong was secure. They said that Mao Zedong had died, Deng Xiaoping was turning to the West and to economic reform, and China needed Hong Kong. During Thatcher's negotiations with Deng, she tried to extend the lease, but Deng Xiaoping said to her, "Madam, I cannot go down in history as a second Li Hongzhang." She then turned to David Wilson, the China scholar who at the time was the governor of Hong Kong, and asked him who Deng Xiaoping was talking about. David Wilson told her he was the Chinese official who in 1898 signed the lease on Hong Kong. It was clear then that Deng Xiaoping did not care what Hong Kong's economic value was. Hong Kong had been transferred to Great Britain as a result of the Opium War, and now it was going back to China. Many times have I said to my Chinese friends, "China is in danger of killing the goose that lays the golden egg," only to have them look me in the eye and say, "Chinese history is full of dead geese. What interests us here is not geese that lay golden eggs, but humiliations that occurred in the past." In short, the old victimization and its consequences still linger and will change the status of Hong Kong, but it will not soon change the status of Taiwan, the division of Korea, or the influence of the U.S. Seventh Fleet. Nevertheless, the shift from mere enrichment to empowerment is clearly on the agenda.

Seen from the perspective of 1995, the agenda accompanying the empowerment of Asia includes many different problems, any one of which has the potential for destabilizing the area and the world as a whole. Experts clearly disagree on the exact contents of this agenda, but the following five issues constitute its core. The first issue is that of Chinese growth rates and the reestablishment of strong economic ties between China and Russia. The second encompasses the claims of "greater China" circulating among the overseas Chinese, who are among the world's richest people. China would like to tap into the skills and assets of these people. It is extremely destabilizing, however, to have China now claiming the allegiance of the overseas Chinese, particularly in Southeast Asia. The third issue is Japan's need, but seeming inability, to shift to a consumer-driven economy. The fourth issue is the unification of Korea, and the fifth issue involves the terms of a future Asia-Pacific balance of power and the role of the United States in maintaining it.

At this point I would like to address the first and third issues regarding China and Japan. In the early 1990s, China had a per capita income of U.S. $547. That was 2.6 percent of the per capita income of the United States (I'm using conservative numbers found

Chalmers Johnson

in the CIA's global atlas). China had a total GNP of U.S. $603.5 billion, or 11.6 percent of the U.S. GNP. China's population of 1.2 billion people, however, is more than four times that of the United States. These numbers mean that China could fairly easily create an economy the same size as that of the United States, yet still have a relatively poor population in terms of per capita income. China, with the world's largest social system, now growing at 10 to 12 percent a year, will be able to produce an economy that is the same size or larger than that of the United States in 10 to 15 years, though its per capita income will be approximately one-sixth of that of the United States or even less. Given the size of China's population, if it achieves a per capita GDP even one-fourth that of the United States—say, approximately U.S. $5,000 (at market exchange rates) which is the size of South Korea's today—China would have an absolute GNP that would be quite a bit larger than that of the United States. Matching the per capita income of South Korea today is not an unrealistic goal for China, particularly given the high growth and savings rates that China has achieved in recent years.

Americans like to believe that economic growth is desirable in and of itself. They also believe that economic growth inevitably leads to democratization. In fact, the Heritage Foundation, a conservative American think tank, states this relationship as if it were a Newtonian law. One of their recent papers stated: "The law of supply and demand is as immutable as the law of gravity. As a country moves up the economic ladder, political freedoms almost always follow." The almost is, of course, a weasel word put in there, but it is the weaseling on which I am going to focus. This remark is explicitly directed to the East Asian NICs (newly industrialized countries), even though most of them are anything but democratic. Moreover, NICs such as South Korea have shown that economic growth tends to slow down as democracy takes hold.

Analytically, American ideologues fail to understand that democracy, seen in purely neutral terms, is a particularly effective way of making decisions under conditions of significant social complexity or heterogeneity. Since economic growth will normally produce greater social differentiation, democracy is a logical response to these conditions. On the other hand, if heterogeneity

201

can be mitigated through fairly equitable income distribution, control of immigration, or an overarching ideology of uniqueness and exceptionalism—practices that are all routine in East Asia—democracy may not be necessary for effective government. Hence, the trade-off between economic growth and democratic government can be delayed or postponed. Currently in East Asia, there are many examples of leaders who claim that Asians do not expect democracy to accompany national wealth because of cultural differences. In fact, the accusation that the United States is imposing its values on Asia in a kind of cultural imperialism has become one of the main issues of U.S.-East Asian diplomacy.

In the past, the Chinese Communist leaders have been wary of using market mechanisms for economic growth precisely because they feared that the Americans were right about market mechanisms leading to the collapse of Communist authoritarianism. One reason that China in recent years has reversed this policy is that the high-growth economies of East Asia—particularly Singapore, Taiwan, and South Korea before the election of President Kim Young Sam—showed that authoritarianism, sometimes disguised by a democratic façade, could indeed be compatible with high levels of per capita income. The decisive change came at the 14th Party Congress in 1992 at which Chinese leaders officially concluded that the Americans were wrong; that is, they concluded that market forces could be used for development without democracy being the end result.

During the Cold War it made sense for the United States to promote China's economic development because it reinforced the strategic triangle with the Soviet Union. Today, however, by giving China most-favored-nation access to the American market, the United States is actively helping China become as big as the United States itself but with no guarantee that its people will be satisfied with a per capita income only a quarter of America's. Nor is there any guarantee that democratic government will ever take place in China. It is time for the United States to start thinking about balancing China's future power and to start recognizing that the relationship between economic development and democracy is not as dependable as the law of gravity. Though it may contradict what is taught in Economics 101, people need to recognize that economic

Chalmers Johnson

development and democracy are not inextricably linked. Even though there may be much about development that might recommend democracy to a society, it should not be assumed that democracy is inevitable.

As for Japan's role in the empowerment of Asia, Japan needs to become a major market for the manufactured goods made in the rest of Asia. Here, the historic contribution that the United States has made to the enrichment of Asia needs to be recognized. It was not in the form of its wars, diplomats, or treaties; instead, it was the U.S. markets. Japan would not have achieved its current level of economic success if the United States had not bought the high quality, low-priced consumer goods, such as videocassette recorders and television sets, that sit in everyone's living room. The United States has provided a ready market for high quality, competitively priced consumer goods first from Japan, from the East Asian NICs, and most recently from Southeast Asia and mainland China. Japan, followed by China and then Taiwan, are the three leading sources of the American trade deficit, an annual deficit that in the case of Japan is $66 billion. American analysts, myself included, have concluded that today's American trade deficit is almost 100 percent attributable to the problem of Japan and East Asia, one that should never have been turned over to lawyers and economists to solve.

The Japanese love to compare the East Asian economy to a V-formation of flying geese with Japan as head goose. This analogy exemplifies one of the interesting tensions in the area today: The Chinese are not at all certain they want to be a goose flying behind Japan. Also, I have long argued with Japanese friends of mine that the problem with their metaphor is that no one ever asks where these geese are flying. My own answer is that they have been flying to Los Angeles. The problem now, however, is that Los Angeles no longer works as a destination, at least not as well as it has in the past.

The role of the United States as East Asia's primary market is coming to an end, not necessarily because the United States is about to close its doors, but because the output of Asia is simply too large. Equally important, the United States also needs to correct its own domestic imbalances and restore its savings and investment, which means it must cut consumption and reduce its

203

trade deficits. The best way to do that would be to impose surcharges on Japanese products entering the American market. Moreover, the surcharges should be placed only on Japanese products because it is chiefly Japan that needs to open its market and because the United States wants to promote other places such as Korea as parts of an emerging balance of power in Asia. To put it another way, the United States does not need to be politically stupid while being economically smart.

The United States also needs to impose high local content requirements on everything sold in the North American market. NAFTA, which gives Mexico preferred access to the American and Canadian markets, also implies a degree of closure of the American market against Japanese dependencies in Southeast Asia. NAFTA has been mis-sold as an economic policy. The demographic trends in Mexico suggest that the United States could easily have another situation like Nicaragua on its southern borders. NAFTA aims to ameliorate demographic trends in Mexico by giving the Mexicans privileged access. That was a good idea. NAFTA should not have been sold as an economic treaty, but as a foreign aid package aimed at stabilizing Mexico and avoiding a second Mexican revolution.

Prime Minister Mahathir of Malaysia is one of the first Asian leaders to understand that the U.S. market will not forever be open to the platforms of Japan in Southeast Asia, and his proposed EAEC is as much a form of pressure on Japan to open its markets as it is retaliation against the United States.

Japan knows what is taking place. In early 1992, the then-head of the Asia Bureau of the Japanese Foreign Ministry, Mr. Sakutaro Tanino, a sophisticated and intelligent man, wrote: "When American Reaganomics are mentioned, their negative side is emphasized because that policy produced the twin deficits—trade and budgetary. But it is also a fact that because of it, the United States emerged as a great absorber of East Asian products. But if the present U.S. government is set to seriously tackle its financial deficits, things will not go as before. In the future the problem will become who will absorb this region's—that is, Asia's—products and support the prosperity of the East Asian economy. I think it will have to be Japan."

Not too long from now, Japan must therefore become a net importer of manufactured goods from Asia. If it fails to do so and forces Asian manufacturers to seek out low end markets in Europe, where the new economies of Eastern Europe are also trying to gain a foothold, it will create massive instabilities in its own region and ultimately around the world. To shift from an essentially producer-driven economy to a consumer-driven economy—that is, from a Victorian economy to an Edwardian one in terms of historical models—Japan will have to undergo major wrenching reforms.

In a sense, the Kobe earthquake may be Japan's much needed wake-up call. What is fascinating about the earthquake is not its 5,000 fatalities, which are very serious, but Japan's inability to respond adequately to it. Here is a nation that profited from the Cold War more than any other nation. In fact, Japan has been the least pleased to see the Cold War end and has tried to perpetuate it as long as possible. Suddenly the Kobe earthquake hits and jolts the Japanese into the awareness that they should quit spending their money on movie companies in Southern California or real estate like Rockefeller Center and that they should stop lending it to Americans who overconsume—in other words, they should start spending their money domestically. Whatever the lessons learned from the Kobe earthquake, Japan will still have to make major reforms. These will include a total overhaul of its land-use laws, a massive program of deregulation, an opening-up to the full pressure of international competition, and an end to its restraints on consumer-centered domestic demand.

Can the Japanese make these changes, and are they prepared to make them in an acceptable time frame? On the first question, the whole experience of the Hosokawa government, August 1993 to April 1994, is instructive. People saw Mr. Hosokawa as a Japanese version of Bill Clinton. *Time* magazine even referred to him as a "southern governor intent on reform." It is hard to think of worse poppycock than what was published by the American press about Morihiro Hosokawa's reign in office after the Liberal Democratic Party (LDP) had ruled for 28 years. Despite promising reforms that even General MacArthur himself could not deliver—in particular his promise to change the relationship between Japan's elected politicians and its permanent state officials—Hosokawa essentially did nothing. He then resigned as the result of a corruption scandal. Hosokawa's resignation as prime minister was useful in bringing a note of realism to the discussion of change in Japan. The Japanese and the Americans know that domestic reform in Japan will not come quickly or without continued internal and external pressure.

The next prime minister of Japan was a Socialist, allied with his natural enemies of the last 40 years, and his position totally mystifies the Americans. How can Mr. Murayama, this sleepy old Socialist who so far has managed to go to Kobe and say nothing more than "Gambatte" ("work hard"), actually be ruling the world's second most productive economy in terms of per capita income?

On the timing of change, the Japanese appear to believe that they still have a few years left in which to maneuver. It seems likely to them that the two turning points will be the American presidential election of 1996, by which time the relative economic decline of the United States will be so marked as to require an end to its business-as-usual trade policies, and the 1997 reversion of Hong Kong to mainland Chinese sovereignty. In 1997, Asia will find out whether China will be able to absorb an entire NIC, whether the process of absorption will be the other way around, or whether the process will lead to chaos. It if leads to chaos—that is, if Hong Kong cannot be governed by the Chinese Communists—this will send an ominous signal around the world. During the next few years Japan must either take some leadership in Asia or else face life in a hostile environment as a big, fat Kuwait that no longer has many foreign friends.

In conclusion, let me stress that the two main actors in the future of the Asia-Pacific region are China and Japan. How their relations will evolve is as clouded by contingencies as is the capacity of the United States to articulate and execute a new post-Communist policy toward the region. The United States can only be certain that with the empowerment of Asia, Asia's international relations will no longer be structured in terms of its responses to the West or to any other set of external powers. Instead, its international relations will be structured in terms of intra-Asian visions and rivalries. Whether the result is an Asian renaissance, disaster, or muddle, it will be made in Asia by Asians and for Asians with the

Americans playing a secondary role. That is, after all, what empowerment means. It is time for Americans to start thinking in those terms.

QUESTION: What do you think is the Japanese capacity to guarantee a trillion dollars worth of American short-term government bonds when they come due?

MR. JOHNSON: The capacity is there; the question is whether a willingness to do so exists. The problem with the academic, economic mind is that it tends to believe that reality works as if it were a mechanism. It fails to remember that the rules are created not by economists, but by lawyers and law schools. The Japanese do not have to lend money to anyone. Furthermore, they are inclined to do it only on their terms. They are also increasingly critical of U.S. overconsumption. In Japan, it is considerably less. There no doubt that Japan underconsumes, but without question, the United States overconsumes. Many Japanese, particularly in the Industrial Bank of Japan, are only too eager to impose IMF rules on the United States on the grounds that U.S. consumption takes up far too great a percentage of U.S. GDP. Any attempt by Japan to restrict the United States will produce mindless rage about how our consumer sovereignty is being infringed upon.

Currently, our savings rate is at its all-time historic low. For all intents and purposes, Americans save nothing. A good illustration of our consumer culture is provided by the media's coverage of the U.S. economic upswing. As the United States began to come out of the recession, the media showed pictures of people walking through shopping malls with voice-overs saying, "They are starting to consume again." And one has to think, "We don't want them to consume again! We want them to save and invest." Serious incentives to save and invest are needed, but the incentives are just not there.

The Japanese underconsume and often describe themselves as "rich Japan, poor Japanese." The Japanese government's viewpoint is that economics are used to enhance national power. The economy is directed not to enrich Japan's citizens, but to increase the wealth of the country. Even when Japanese describe their own country as "rich Japan, poor Japanese," they see the United States as a system of "private wealth and public poverty." On the asymmetries between the two economies, the Japanese are pretty accurate.

As a result, the Japanese do not necessarily regard the United States as a good investment anymore. They have taken a huge beating over exchange rates, since many of their investments continue to be valued in dollars. Hence, the United States always has the threat of simply expropriating the Japanese by devaluing the American dollar. This would not really affect Americans unless they wanted to go to Japan or wanted to invest in Japan. At the same time, Japanese investment in the United States may become less of an issue in the future, as Japanese funds will likely be absorbed by Asia in increasing amounts. Chinese demand for financing, for example, is limitless. I sometimes think that the United States has finally found a way to keep the Japanese preoccupied—by assigning them the economic development of China.

Also, as mentioned earlier, the Kobe earthquake is likely to have a considerable impact on the Japanese. The earthquake is the catalyst by which the Japanese public is now beginning to appreciate fully the fact that their own country also needs investment. Japan is not overcrowded the way that Hong Kong and Holland are. One can palpably taste the Japanese desire for better housing in their country. Meanwhile, in the United States the issue of bringing deficits under control has finally caught the attention of American politics at the last possible moment. American citizens are beginning to understand that it may not be possible to continue financing the American government with someone else's savings.

QUESTION: Could the Peninsula Hotel in Hong Kong and the fact that it is fully booked for June 1997 be symbolic of what the Hong Kong people think about Hong Kong's return to China?

MR. JOHNSON: The argument can be made either way. That is why China is such a wonderful and classical enigma. The old order in China is passing, as it inevitably must. China will not be able to reverse the process that has begun, even if there is some repression in the wake of Deng Xiaoping. Hong Kong is not really going back to China so much as all of southeastern, seaboard China is turning into Hong Kong.

Most of the Hong Kong population are apolitical, are committed to making money, and will try to adjust to the commissars that will be arriving. The main message I want to convey is that there is an enormous danger of what the Chinese refer to as *jingji zhiyi*—that is, "economism," which means giving priority to economics. We in America may be the last genuine materialists in the world in that we still believe that at bottom, all decisions are economic. The one thing that soon becomes apparent about the Chinese is that they do not believe that statement.

The Chinese have offered many signs that they are not driven entirely by economics. They are extremely shrewd politically and are the oldest practitioners of statecraft on earth. The Chinese have laid claim to all of the South China Sea as part of their territorial waters, which has caused trouble at once with Vietnam, the Philippines, and Malaysia. More important, however, China's claim raises questions about Japan because all of Japan's oil goes through the South China Sea. With this claim, China is essentially saying, "The Americans, whether they know it or now, are going home. They are going home as surely as the Russians finally went home from Germany. The future of the world is between China and Japan. With this claim, we Chinese are putting in place a little necessary leverage for future use against these other smart people in Northeast Asia."

I find it extremely interesting that the greatest source of long-term capital in California right now is mainland Chinese money. Laundered through Hong Kong and Taiwan, this money is used to buy things in California. In Southern California, communities east of Pasadena are very wealthy Chinese communities. This fact interests me because while Americans are desperately trying to invest in China, rich Chinese are taking their wealth and investing it in America. They are parking their money outside the country for safekeeping until they know for certain the direction the wind is blowing in China. China is a case of investor beware. In fact, many people believe that the Chinese are about to take the

Japanese to the greatest laundry ever. After all, the Chinese have gotten the Japanese to invest in China and to transfer technology.

Clearly devoted to the principle of *jingji zhiyi*, the Japanese believe that they can so draw the Chinese into a complex web of economic relations that the Chinese will ultimately put those interests ahead of any political interest. The Japanese believe that the Chinese will eventually adjust to what is now a reality, which is the Greater East Asian Co-Prosperity Sphere. It is important to understand, however, that this co-prosperity sphere is different from the one Japan tried to build in the 1930s and the 1940s. For example, it has not been built at the point of a bayonet, and that is an important difference. Moreover, this one does offer the opportunity for genuine prosperity.

Currently, many newspapers are putting obituaries for Deng Xiaoping into their computers. One of the immediate consequences of Deng Xiaoping's death will be greater domestic repression in the regime's attempt to avoid *luan*—that is, confusion. To avoid chaos, China will try to maintain control as much as possible. At the same time, however, a shrewd Japanese editor said to me, "Yes, post-Deng China will be repressive, but it will also be fake repression; that is, two or three significant people will be thrown to the wolves as a warning to everyone else, but China's leaders will not want to reverse current trends." It is fair to say that the Chinese are enjoying their growing wealth. In short, the future of China and Asia is yet to be decided. I simply do not believe that any of us knows what is going to happen.

NARRATOR: We have been privileged to have Professor Chalmers Johnson and appreciate him sharing his insights on Japan and China with us.